THE
FIRST YEAR
OF
PRIESTHOOD

THE
FIRST YEAR
OF
PRIESTHOOD

David K. O'Rourke

AN OSV SOURCE BOOK
Series Editor, Albert J. Nevins, M.M.

Our Sunday Visitor, Inc.
Huntington, Indiana 46750

Nihil Obstat:
Rev. Ernest R. Martinez, S.J.
Censor Librorum

Imprimatur:
✠ John S. Cummins
Bishop of Oakland
June 12, 1978

ISBN: 0-87973-832-4
Library of Congress Catalog Number: 78-60486

Cover Design by James E. McIlrath

Published, printed and bound in the U.S.A. by
Our Sunday Visitor, Inc.
Noll Plaza
Huntington, Indiana   46750

832

Dedication

Training for ministry today is commonly a team effort. Many of the ideas presented in this work are the product of collective efforts in introducing men and women to the work of the Church. Ideas and theories are tied together one to another like the links in a chain, and acknowledging the work of one colleague carries with it am implicit thank you to his or her co-workers.

Specifically I would like to thank Fr. Leo Thomas, O.P., former Professor of Pastoral Theology at the Dominican School of Theology and Graduate Theological Union, Berkeley, California, who with me began the program that gave rise to this work, and who also provided much of the conceptual framework on the process of entry; Shirley Cooper, M.S., Chief Psychiatric Social Worker, Department of Psychiatry, Mt. Zion Hospital, San Francisco, with whom several years of consultation on supervision accounts for much of the good in the sections on supervision; Dr. Edward Burke, Associate Clinical Professor of Psychiatry, University of California, San Francisco, and a colleague in the program, whose experiences in the adolescent drug ward of the Langley Porter Neuropsychiatric Clinic helped provide a model for coping with pastoral crises. I am also indebted to the late Chaplain Thomas Klink, Director of the Division of Religion and Psychiatry, The Menninger Foundation, Topeka, Kansas, for a most helpful consultation on the role of intimacy in the life of the newly ordained. Special thanks go to Alice Mazzucchi, Fran Mullen and Joan Wendell for typing and re-typing the manuscript.

Contents

CHAPTER ONE

beginning pastoral work

Process of Entry into Pastoral Work

Getting started is not easy. No matter whether the starting be for a physician, a tightrope walker, a married couple, or a new priest, the process of starting out is not easy. And the beginning period often proves to be anything but a honeymoon. This is especially true of the newly ordained priest, because his life is so complex and the stakes are so high.

This book is about getting started. It is about the process of entry into pastoral work, a study of what happens to newly ordained priests as they move from their seminary studies into priestly work. Let it be said from the beginning that a lot happens; it is a busy time. The events during this period have a powerful effect on the new priest and color the course of his ministry, and consequently affect the people he serves. Because this beginning period seems to last about a year, our study is about the first year of pastoral work.

This first year is a critical time. It is a year of transition and change, of adaptation and beginnings. There is the transition from the role of the student to the role of the practitioner, from the role of the learner who does little pastoral work to the role of the fully functioning priest who is trying to put learning to work. There is a change in status from the low status and restricted state of the seminarian to the higher status and considerable privilege of the priesthood. There is a great change in the type and intensity of the expectations that people have of a man once he is ordained. There is change in his visibility, for he goes from being a private person to being the bearer of a role that is much in the public eye. There is change in the quality of his home life, for the rectory presents a living situation that is quite different from that of the seminary.

In addition to this change and transition, there is much that is completely new. There are significant experiences which the new priest encounters for the first time. To begin with, he is moving into a life work in which service to others is central. People will place demands on him assuming that they have the right to make these demands. People will ask his advice and, at least in the area of his public role, defer to his authority. He will experience an ancient and sacred role from the inside, and may feel overwhelmed.

These new experiences require adaptation. The new priest must shift his way of doing things in several significant areas. He must learn a new way of relating to people. Heretofore, he has related as a private person but from now on there will be a new dimension that goes beyond his own person. He must learn how to cope with the expectations that both his people and the Church as an institution place on their priests. He will have to learn how to adjust to a role that is not only public but highly visible.

During this year the beginning priest is establishing the ground rules for the exercise of his priesthood. The way he responds to requests for help, to crisis and to the unexpected, and the way he deals with relationships in his living situations, in his work and in personal encounters, will have a deep effect on him. In his response to this new life he is adapting himself in and by that very response. The ways he responds will form patterns that will stay with him.

The first year is as difficult as it is important. To begin with, the tasks the new priest must master are numerous and demanding. In addition, there are crises to be weathered. These crises, as we will point out, prove capable of causing him considerable self-doubt and vocational insecurity. In the following chapters we will examine both the beginning tasks and the crises as a way of understanding why the beginning period is so critical and difficult.

Three Focal Points in Methodology

Several aspects of this beginning period need explaining in order to clarify the method we will use in this study. The first of these is time. The duration or time-lapse in the entry period is important. The second is the notion of process. The entry into pastoral work is not a single event, but a lengthy process. What we mean by process needs explanation. The third is the fact that the priest's new life is both structured and intelligible. What these structures are and how they affect the beginning priest need explaining. We will look into each of these elements—time, process, and structure—in turn.

Time proves to be an important issue for the beginning priest. As he begins his new work he must cope with a new identity, with a different set of human relationships, and with many different and often quite new situations. Learning to cope with these requires time; it does not occur overnight. The new priest has much to learn, and chief among these is a new way of learning. This new way is a process, not a single event or a series of isolated events. It is a continuum grounded in the human experience of one individual. In this process the element of time and the duration of this period are important. Only during a protracted period of time can he encounter the people, situations, and seasons that foster his learning. He has a need for the raw material of pastoral experiences, for impressions to be established and then challenged or reinforced, for responses and reactions to be sorted out and evaluated.

Further, and this is most important, it is only with the passage of time that the critical issues develop and surface. Ordinarily, the chief crises of entry into pastoral work do not manifest themselves during the first six months and, as we shall see, there is a time-related reason why they do not. When they do surface, the manner of their surfacing has an important time component to it.

The second aspect of the period of adaptation we noted is that it

13

is a process. Process entails continuity. It does not bespeak just an event or a number of isolated events but a series of events played out over a period of time. It does not involve only the events but the people in these events and what happens to them as they experience the events, and the effect these relationships have on those involved in them.

Process bespeaks time, change, and growth. In the case of the seminarian who is becoming a priest, it bespeaks a long time, long enough to entail considerable change and growth. From the time that he first begins his studies for the priesthood officially as a seminarian up to the time of his ordination and the beginning of his first assignment, five or six years will go by. The length of time itself does not constitute the process. What we mean by process is more appropriately described by what takes place during these years, the socialization of the seminarian into that particular part of the Church's life that will be his.

In addition, we can speak of being process-minded. This connotes an approach which is questioning and analytic, not merely accepting. Part of this comes from the belief that what is going on is both identifiable and intelligible. It means that we can actually understand what is going on. We can understand what the individual has in his own personal history and makeup and how this affects his way of relating. We can identify his strengths, his weaknesses, and his way of coping with people and events. We can understand the structures and dynamics of the settings in which he is ministering and the ways in which he is being incorporated into or kept out of its circle of insiders. We can identify the expectations, both stated and unstated, that those involved in pastoral situations have of each other. Finally, as he goes through the course of his pastoral work, we can help him see how he is interacting with the people and structures he encounters and how this interaction affects him.

In addition, to be process-minded means seeing these processes as subject to control. With the ability to control a process of development, we can set standards of quality for that development. We can speak not only about the process of becoming a priest, but the process of becoming an effective priest. We can see that the knowledge given by an analysis of a pastoral situation and the people in it, both the priest and those with whom he is working, allows us to figure out what to do in order to work for pastoral effectiveness.

Granted this is an idealized and abstract view of the notion of process. The point here, however, is that the process of entry into pastoral work is both identifiable and controllable. In the past, many clergy entered their work and, either praying to God or trusting to luck, or both, hoped it would work out. When it did they were relieved. When it did not they were often scarred.

There is an alternative to this haphazard manner of entry. With an educated awareness of what is going on during the process of entry, it is not necessary to trust to luck. The situation, the circumstances affecting it and its goals, can be grasped and appropriate means for achieving these goals can be devised. Both success and failure can be understood and their causes pinpointed. Invariably this pinpointing narrows the focus, and with it, the newcomer's sense of responsibility. Feelings of global responsibility are overwhelming. Pinpointed responsibilities, on the other hand, can more easily be coped with. An analytic approach to the process of entry into pastoral work measurably increases the chances of success in that work.

One of the ways in which we can grasp the notion of process is to consider the difference between adaptation and adjustment. This use of these words may be arbitrary but it proves helpful. Adjustment can be seen as slight and external modifications of behavior and ways of doing things in order to get along. Adaptation, at least as we use it here, refers to a more fundamental change, a shifting of attitudes, values, and behavior, and a change stimulated by the need to survive. We can note this in the case of Father B, whose mouth frequently started operating before his brain. Assigned to a parish, he adjusted to what he considered to be the eccentricities of the pastor and staff. However, he was vocal in noting that these were eccentricities and that his way was better. After an angry exchange, the pastor informed the bishop that he wanted Father B removed. Father B, deeply shaken by this unexpected turn of events, went to his new assignment with the realization that "I've got to learn to keep my mouth shut." For the sake of survival he was changing his behavior and no longer adjusted to his surroundings, but adapted.

It is a commonplace principle in educational theory that learning entails adaptation. The process of entry into pastoral work is a process of learning and adaptation. On the most fundamental level it is a lesson in survival and, as the numbers of priests leaving their ministry during this beginning phase indicates, it is a lesson that is not always learned. In addition, on a qualitatively higher level, the entry process is also a lesson in working effectively.

Adaptation is sufficiently difficult that most people would skip it if they could. Adaptation bespeaks change. All change entails some loss, and loss involves pain. Most people would prefer to avoid a painful process if it were possible. For the beginning priest it is not really possible. A successful entry into his work requires that he learn to adapt. This adaptation is not the result of a choice which he makes at some particular point, but rather is the response to the realities he encounters in his work. These realities serve as stimuli which demand an adaptive response. It would be foolish to assume that the adaptive responses of all beginning priests will be the same. Just as each individual is different, so his learning and adaptation is going to be different. What survival means varies from individual to individual. So does the definition of personally satisfying work. Nonetheless, we can note that there are issues around which the process of adaptation focuses. Some of them become crisis issues. There are tasks to be accomplished by the beginning priest. There are personal needs that have to be met. In each of these situations the individual will respond in his own way but we can predict that whatever the way might be, he will, in fact, respond. We can identify that response.

The third element we mentioned above as being significant in this period of adaptation is the fact that the priest is entering into a life both structured and intelligible. He has not come out of a vacuum, but has been trained within the structured context of a Catholic seminary. He has been given an education with its own proper content and proper methodology. He has been given a personal formation through the style of life he's led in the seminary.

His new work is equally structured. He does not serve his people in a fluid or shapeless manner, but within a role consisting of standardized relationships and expectations. To begin with there is the sacramental life of the Church. The Sacraments involve him with his people at very significant times in their lives—birth, marriage, illness, and death. Further, they involve him in set ways. What he does at these times and how he does it are already established by traditions, ritual, and the expectations of the people. How he and his people relate to each other on these occasions is also set down. No matter what the style of the liturgy at a wedding, for example, no matter whether it be a traditional wedding with organ and many attendants, or a modern wedding with guitar music and simple dress, he is still the Church's public witness. He plays a visible and public role in the ceremony, and people view a public and religious official in a way different from their view of another private person.

Expectations of the priest come also from the lived religious experience of the people. In the course of living their faith they come in contact with priests as pastors, teachers, and confessors, as chaplains in schools and hospitals, and in other similar roles. They meet sisters in schools and hospitals. The people interact with clergy and religious. They like some, they dislike others, and because of the key role the priest plays in the life of Catholic people they remember their likes and dislikes. These memories, both positive and negative, friendly or fearful and angry, are part of the experience they bring to any relationship with the new priest. For better or worse, these experiences are as real as the enthusiasm and ideals of the newly ordained priest, and they will affect his ministry as much.

Formative Role of Educational and Training Process

The new priest must learn to cope with the public's view of the priesthood. What a priest does and what he does not do, how he

17

acts, dresses and talks, the way he relates to people, the places he goes and does not go, are part of the people's view of the priest. No matter whether these impressions, expectations, and structures are appropriate or not, whether they are consistent or inconsistent, whether the new priest approve of them or not, they are real and must be recognized for the realities they are. They are realities which shape and direct his person and his work. They loom very large in the life of anyone who works both for and in the Church, and have a formative effect on his life. Unfortunately, they are not always recognized for the formative structures they are.

In a classical work on professional education Charlotte Towle notes that most professionals have a good grasp of Freudian psychodynamics. However, in "The Learner in Education for the Professions" (University of Chicago, 1954, p. 23), she points out that they really do not understand much educational psychology. The basic human drives and needs are more commonly understood than what goes on in the individual as he learns. And yet, the process of learning proves to be as interesting as it is important. What the individual goes through as he moves from the student's situation to the situation of a practicing professional will color the way in which he practices his profession. Quite properly, educators for the several professions are insistent that their students master the skills and knowledge proper to the profession. It is important to note, however, that the professional educator's insistence, as such, enters into the educational process just as effectively as does the focus of the learning. We have found that the effect the educational and training process has on the priest in training can be as important as what he learns. Sometimes it is more important. Many an old priest has forgotten the content of his seminary courses, but he still remembers vividly, sometimes painfully, the discipline and rigor with which they were taught.

In this book we will look at this process. We will look at newly ordained priests as they go through their first year and will do so by drawing largely on their recorded experiences. We will look at what actually happened as they began their pastoral work.

There will be several points of focus. First, we will examine the situation of the priest as he begins his work. This will require an understanding of the forces that are at work in him; namely, the life he has led in preparation for his new role and work, the buildup to his ordination, and the personal agenda he brings with him. We will then look at the several tasks that face the beginning priest. The degree of success he attains in mastering these tasks, as we shall see, affects not only his own sense of competence but, more important, his questions about whether or not he made the right move in becoming a priest. As we look into these tasks we will also be looking at his priestly work itself, such as job description, personnel questions, etc., both from the point of view of its structures and the personal issues it arouses in the individual priest. This raises questions of how he gets along with people. Finally we will look into the major crisis which proves to be the critical and pivotal issue in the initial phase of pastoral work.

As we noted our study will draw on the recorded experiences of priests in the process of beginning their pastoral work. We will follow themes rather than give longitudinal biographies of individuals. From the experiences of the individuals we will draw out the themes and issues that arise during the beginning phase of pastoral work rather than trace the learning and living process of any particular individual or individuals. Our reason for this method is twofold. First, the several issues and crises that surface do so with surprising similarity. The variation from one individual to another is not that great. Further, the individuals themselves note that these themes prove sufficiently important that they merit consideration in themselves. Our second reason is that this method allows us to cite actual situations which, because of their commonness, will not be personally identifying. In all cases the identifying circumstances have been changed to further assure anonymity.

Seminary Training Different

In seeking to understand the entry into the ministry we are tempted to do so by comparing training for the priesthood with educational methods common in other professions. Medicine, law, social service, *et. al.*, have systems of training, certification, and processes of entry. But the priest's situation is basically different. Comparing his situation to that of other professionals leads to distortion. The distortion comes about because these comparisons focus on the study and work. The seminarian does work and study, but he does much more. He is also engaged in a process sufficiently involving that it can be called a life-stage. The word seminarian does not only say what the young man does, it also says, on a much deeper level, who he is.

Erik Erikson, in *Gandhi's Truth* (New York: Norton & Co., 1969, p. 37), contrasts "the almost vindictive monotony of Judean-Christian strictures, by which we gain or forfeit salvation, by the formation of one consistently virtuous character almost from cradle to grave" with the succession of notably different life-styles of the Hindu world. Seminary training followed by the entry into the priesthood is more like the different and successive life-styles of the Hindu world than they are similar to the American, professional training model. Why is this so? To understand we must look at the nature of seminary life. Especially we will look at the formative influence of social structures so common that they are overlooked.

The seminary may be seen as an educational institution, but if we look at it as a whole and look to its social roots we will see soon enough that the seminary is modeled on the monastery. The monastery of the western monastic tradition is the source and model of the Tridentine seminary, the seminary which still is functional today, albeit with modifications. Granted, many seminaries today are a far cry from the straight-laced institutions of a generation ago. But there is more to a monastery than long corridors and rigorous discipline. It is primarily a symbol of deliberate and radical change in a man's way of life. No matter whether the living takes place in a cloister or in an apartment complex the symbolic dimension can still be functional. To understand this we must dismiss pictures of robes and buildings from our minds, and in their place try to understand the human and social dynamics.

The monastery is counter-cultural and monastic life is deviant; they institutionalize a withdrawal from accustomed civilian life. Seen as a preparation for the priesthood, this deviant life prepares the beginning priest for the prophetic role he must exercise in his priestly life, that of shaping norms and values for society rather than fitting into the norms and values that society has developed through moral compromise. Those seminarians who are involved in counter-cultural activities, protest movements of one sort or another, are doing no more than manifesting the formation and shaping they are receiving in this quite formative institution. Church officials, often dismayed by the activities of their seminarians, overlook the relationship between the formative power of the at least vestigially monastic life-style of the seminary and the actions of their seminarians. Whether or not the formative power manifests itself in areas as diverse as social action, abstract academics, or artistic production, it is a united manifestation in that each activity uses the monastic base as a supportive place in which or from which to work. In each case, the thrust is counter-cultural. Preserving the past, changing the present, or bringing about the future are all ways of countering what is going on here and now.

Official dismay at seminarians' counter-cultural activities, coupled with the desire for greater professional competence, is leading some dioceses and religious groups to change education so that seminarians will become more like other American professional students. Living arrangements are less formalized. Programs of study are less structured. Seminarians are being enrolled with increasing frequency in the seminary complexes that are being established in our urban centers. In part the seminarians will be students of theology, largely indistinguishable from other students, and in part they will be pastoral apprentices under the direction of some priest charged with giving them ecclesial know-how. It remains to be seen whether, or how, this system will affect the counter-cultural aspect of seminary formation which, at least on a structural level, supports the prophetic dimension of priestly life.

The transition from *being a seminarian* to *being a priest* is not primarily a move from one part to another part of a continuum, like the change from being a medical student to being a doctor. It is a change in life-style, from a withdrawn and preparatory life-style to involvement and service that belongs to the priesthood. It is a radical shift, a jolting about-face, for it means leaving behind one wholly involving life-style and taking on a new, different, and even more involving one.

Unfortunately, unlike in Hindu society, we are not effective at providing help in this transition period. The newly ordained priest can and should become an explorer, the pilgrim seeking out his God through sounding the depths of his new life. Unfortunately, he too often becomes not an explorer, but a wanderer anxiously seeking an understanding of what is happening to him while, simultaneously, seeking some protection and support in the face of situations, events, and people that threaten to overwhelm him.

Source of Study

This volume has grown out of a program designed to assist the beginning priest make the transition from the seminary to pastoral work, from one life-style to the other life-style. It has grown out of the recognition that the entry into pastoral work is a difficult process. This realization was made concrete in a program designed to support the beginning priest as he enters into his new life and work. The program utilizes four basic elements.

First, there is a challenge to the individual in the form of the demands of his new pastoral setting. All that he has been learning and all in which he has invested very much is now to be put to the test. The need to do well, to protect the investment he has made through years of work, and the decision for ordination is very real indeed.

Following upon the challenge there is, second, an analysis of it. Pastoral situations are intelligible. It is possible to understand what is going on. It is possible to determine what help people are looking for. It is possible to help the beginning priest see how he relates to people, to see both his strengths and his weaknesses, and to understand the dynamics of the situation in which he finds himself. This is a relatively new way of looking at things. Up to now it has been common to accept human interaction as a given, much as, a few centuries ago, the forces of nature were accepted as a given. But as the forces of nature can be understood and channeled, so can the dynamics of human interaction be understood.

This understanding is put to work through a designed response, the third of the elements that enter into the program. Anticipating what will and will not work in pastoral situations, we can choose means and methods accordingly. Drawing on his known personal strengths and the institutional strengths of his priesthood, the beginning priest can respond effectively. He can also learn how to utilize the resources of the community in which he finds himself, whether or not these resources are religious, medical, educational, economic, or social. Drawing on theory and past experience, both his own and that of the Church, and utilizing the resources at his disposal, he can be helped to design a response that will work.

A fourth element that enters into the program is personal support. Getting started in any work situation is difficult. It can be especially difficult for priests. The beginning priest cannot be expected to start off completely on his own. He needs to be helped just as do other professional people. He needs the assistance of work superiors and peers in moving into his new work. The beginning priest needs to know that the difficulties he experiences really are objective difficulties, not the result of some lack on his part. He needs to know how others perceive him, both positively and negatively, and how their perceptions differ from his own. He needs moral support and the assurance that some sort of personal support will be forthcoming when the going gets rough. He needs also to test his own perceptions about the stress and anxiety of pastoral work against the perceptions of his peers and superiors. He needs someone to teach him how things are done in his particular work situation, what the standards are for acceptable performance, whether his own performance is acceptable or not, and how to make his performance acceptable by commonly accepted standards. He needs the knowledge that when situations arise which threaten to overwhelm him, regardless of circumstances or fault, that someone or something will defend him. All this support requires help and understanding from others. The need for this support is real, and he is entitled to receive it. To give him less than this is to set him up for considerable stress and possible failure. One value of the training program from which this volume has grown is that it provided its participants with this support, especially with regard to their relationship with their work superiors. The fact that the beginning priests were participants in an officially sanctioned training program lessened the sense of being the lowest man in rank.

These four elements—challenge, analysis, planned response, and personal support—are at the heart of what we have found to be a successful method for assisting priests to begin their work. How these enter into the process of entry into pastoral work will be explained throughout the course of this volume.

CHAPTER TWO

the

starting point

Formative Role of Seminary

The process of entry into the priesthood begins in the seminary where the priest is trained. This period of seminary education plays a major role in shaping his understanding of the Church and of the priesthood. On an experiential level by what it requires of him during his years of formation, it trains him in a way of presenting himself and of responding to others. He brings this training to his priestly work, and it has an effect on his work.

The seminary is not just a place. In addition, and even more important, it is an institution, a network of human interactions, of relationships, services, duties, and expectations. It may revolve around a single educational and living situation, or it may involve a complex of different faculties, separate living quarters, and varied enrollments. But we can look at either of these as institutions. Like any institution, the seminary has its structured ways of relating to people and of doing things. Its procedures and its responses, both to its staff and to those it serves, are institutionalized. Like any institution, and by the very definition of being institutionalized, it has a life independent of the people who go to make it up.

We can see what this means if we look at the different ways in which the seminary views its students. To begin with, it sees them narrowly as students. This means that it sees them not in the light of their total personalities but insofar as they are there to gain a certain amount of specialized knowledge. From this point of view, the seminary as an institution relates to its students precisely as students. It is a teacher and its purpose is to teach its students.

In addition, the seminary sees its students as potential Church workers. It trains young men to fit into the structure of the Church in the way a good worker does. The seminary also knows that among its students are some on whom the responsibilities for high-level leadership will fall. It initiates the process of competition and filtering that brings this leadership to the surface.

The seminary also sees its students as one part of its constituency. Like any educational institution, the seminary is responsible to a constituency whose likes and opinions it must take into consideration. The constituency consists, first, of the student body itself. The seminary must maintain a credibility among its students or risk discontent or smaller numbers. The other segment of the constituency is the local Church, especially the bishop, diocesan officials, and the more vocal priests and laity. Those who run the seminary, both its appointed officials and others who shape its policies and actions, end up often balancing the two parts of their constituency.

The act of balancing, the parts of a constituency is, in turn, a powerful teacher. The students observe this juggling act and, for better or worse, learn from it. From the reactions of the administration and faculty they learn what constitutes problems and how problems are created. They learn how problems are looked at and they learn an initial response to troubling and troubled situations.

What goes on in the seminary is often of interest to its constituencies. Many clergy, both secular and religious, have feelings about the way students are being taught at the seminary, and they make their feelings known. Their interest is well founded for they must depend on the assistance of the students who come out of the seminary. Now and then they have to explain to themselves and to the laity published accounts of seminary activities. They also realize that the attitudes and beliefs inculcated in the students are going to be brought with the students as soon as they are ordained and sent to their parishes. As a result, they are interested in the seminary, and this interest is reasonable.

It is most important that they make their interest known. They can and often do form a vocal bloc which comes across to the administrators of the seminary as a force which must be taken into consideration. The seminary officials are called on to exercise a considerable amount of political adeptness in balancing and coping with the pressures that are put on them.

By observing these dynamics the students learn several important lessons which will mark their priesthood. First, they learn a need for the fine art of psychological self-defense. Seminary administrators—like other educators today—are a harried group. They live under the pressure of constant evaluation by their constituencies. These priests approach their constituencies on the defensive and the students note this posture. The influence of the seminary professors and administrators is great because they are the priests most present and visible to the seminarians.

In addition, the students pick up the lesson of responsibility. It is a rare seminarian who goes through the formation process feeling indifferent to the Church, its moral directives, the effect it has on the lives of its people, and its impact on society. Whether he approves or disapproves of Church teachings, he feels responsible for them. This sense of responsibility may manifest itself in support or by opposition to the Church, but very rarely does it ever manifest itself by absence and indifference.

Another lesson the seminarian learns is one of authority or power. He sees that as long as the seminary officials keep their jobs they have the right to make decisions. He also learns by observation that it is normal and expected for a person with authority to fight to maintain that right, and that a loss of power is a defeat to be avoided. Increasingly, others have the right to be involved in or even veto decisions, but the seminarian learns that the officials who play

27

their cards right and act intelligently are often able to preserve their authority.

The seminary teaches its students how to cope with a variety of pressures and demands by exposing them to a highly sensitive area of the life of the Church, the seminary itself. The seminary today is no ivory tower. It is a hotbed of ideas and one of the most symbolic vehicles for actualizing the hopes, changes, reactions, and fears of the Church. By his exposure to this institution, the seminarian learns lessons that may well have a greater effect on his priesthood than what he learns in the classroom.

It would be impossible for exposure to the seminary not to have a strong effect on its students. Perhaps the chief reason for this is that the seminary as an institution tries to influence all aspects of the student's life. It is not just a school he is attending. It is much more like a foster parent who is spelling out the requisites for becoming part of the family. In order to belong, all that the seminarian is and does is subject to approval. All the aspects of his life, his learning, his living arrangements, his leisure activities and the relationships he develops are areas on which judgment falls. Catholic seminary education takes the theoretical view that the student's entire life is connected with his priesthood. Therefore, this whole life should be affected by the religious formation and education he receives in the seminary. There is the belief that the integration of his private life into his seminary training requires direction and pressure. Even where students make their own living arrangements there is usually the expectation that they will have to account for how well they are doing. Without denying that the future situation may be different we should note that at present Catholic seminary education still presupposes the integration of all aspects of the student's life into his training and the appropriateness of judging all aspects of his life.

This method of seminary training has major advantages to it. It has achieved one of the prime goals of the Counter-Reformation, the establishment of an educated and celibate secular clergy. This goal is so vast in its implications that it is often overlooked. The seminary method also screens out individuals who have no capacity for asceticism or service, another important advantage.

There are also disadvantages to our current method of seminary education. Chief among these is the establishment of a climate of stress. Educational psychologists tell us that stress breeds its own form of learning. This learning is not as much creative as it is a response to the demands of the teacher. A student under stress will go through the motions he assumes he is to perform. Unfortunately, this sort of learning can be pastorally disastrous. It does not prepare the seminarian for his pastoral work. The automatic response he learns in order to cope with the seminary will not really fit the situation in a parish. In fact, responding automatically to a situation of stress can prove more a liability than an asset in his work. He will often have to cope with stress, but a stress which comes from crisis situations in the lives of his people. Learning how to cope with his teachers' demands may not prepare him to act when the bride's mother suffers an attack during a wedding rehearsal, or when a heckler shouts him down during a sermon. At these times of crisis his ability to think on his feet becomes a must. This means that he needs to know how to respond creatively. One of the tasks a student must learn in his first year of ministry is to move from the automatic responses he learned in the classroom to the creative responses that are necessary for effective pastoral work.

Another lesson he has learned which proves harmful in his pastoral work is the need to approach his people defensively. As noted above, seminary administrators are often on the defensive, and they have been the seminarian's prime priestly models during his years of education. To protect themselves, to survive in their work and in their administrative positions, many seminary officials respond cautiously, reflectively—with much awareness of how their responses will affect others. They are models of defensive reaction. What the student learns from them is that spontaneity and candor are not as valuable as the reflected response.

The seminarian also learns that official or public responses and private responses differ. The candid response, namely, his own estimation of some situation and how it affects him personally, he may share with chosen friends. In public, his responses are conditioned and expected ones. Again, this becomes problematic. The student is learning that who and what he is as a person is a private matter which is not to be brought into the public forum. In public he is a representative of and spokesman for the Church.

Separating his public and private selves is a liability. One of his chief pastoral tasks will be community building, and in community building, who he is as a person is of prime importance. His means for building the Church are not only his specialized skills, knowledge, or the work he can do for his people, but also, and perhaps even more so, his ability to show how he has integrated Christian beliefs into his own life.

Alongside the seminarian's "official" life are the relationships he maintains by choice with other students and, on occasion, with some of the faculty. From these relationships he learns much, but what he learns often differs from his official learning as friendship differs from business relationships. He learns the meaning of support, acceptance and affection, lessons which can teach him much about the role of a pastor.

From his chosen counselors and confessors he can learn what it means to be forgiven and accepted. This does not mean that all counselors and confessors are equally accepting, but the chances are that he will find ones who fit his description of kindness. As long as they fit his description, then he can have what for him is a valid experience of it. Through the course of his studies the average seminarian has access to a priest as a confessor. From this relationship the student receives not only those benefits that are derived from a confessional situation, but also he learns how to be a confessor. He learns one of the most important roles he will be fulfilling, that of helping people with wrongdoing and their feelings about it.

Compared to the organization-oriented roles he learns from his teachers and the seminary administrators, the confessional role is usually a more person-oriented and compassionate role. It is not uncommon for a seminarian to discuss with his confessor something from his own personal life that he has found troubling. Because the word gets around about which confessors are both sound and humane, the average student has the opportunity to experience an intelligent and compassionate response to his situation. What he usually learns, is that his own human frailties are not all that different from other peoples'. He learns that it is possible for another human being to know of them and still respond to him fraternally.

The difficulty with this good lesson is that it is learned in an atmosphere of secrecy and confidentiality. The student's experience of this humane response is a secret experience; it does not take place in a public forum. Unfortunately, the public forum is designated for administrative responses and the communication of specialized skills and knowledge. The seminarian thus receives the institutionally communicated view that kindness and compassion take place behind closed doors, whereas in public one is formal and administrative. It is part of the model to which he is exposed, and it will likely affect the exercise of the ministry.

Relationships with chosen friends present another unofficial but very important way of learning how to relate as a pastor. The seminarian has the opportunity to make good and lasting friendships. In these, he can establish comfortable relationships, ones in which he will not be required to adapt in ways which would cause him to muster his defenses, but ones in which he experiences trust, comfort, acceptance, and affection. These relationships, once seen as relevant to the student's pastoral life, serve as a powerful model for pastoral effectiveness.

Side by side with these relationships of friendship is the broader context of peer relationships. The latter are not always either friendly or supportive. An important aspect of peer relationship is its competitive dimension. Students are encouraged to do both well *and* better than others. It is a rare seminary that does not have the walls of its entry area lined with the portraits of those of its graduates who have succeeded. Success here means having attained ecclesiastical authority. Whether the portraits be of bishops or religious superiors, they are of those who have made it to the top.

The encouragement the students receive to do better is quite different from the excelling that is generally sought in other educational and professional schools. The motivation comes from an institution that is not good at providing positive outlets for drive and initiative, or (using more psychological terms) for aggressive instincts. The seminary's competitive spirit is combined in a curious manner with a process of leveling. The student leader who stands out in a way that brings him official approval is the student who visibly, enthusiastically, and successfully fits into the system. The seminarian who does well in his studies, who is liked by his peers, who is involved in pastoral activities, and who is good at advancing the institution's goals will feel the hand of approval on his shoulder.

However, the sort of excelling which initiates comparisons between the student and his elders, especially those which suggest that the seminarian would be better in a particular job than its present occupant, is more apt to bring on disapproval than approval. The seminary is a training ground for generals but it is also the generals' training ground for the rank and file. Most authorities are more interested in assistants than in replacements, human nature being what it is.

The seminary is especially affected by this situation, for it is the training ground for a much more closed system of life than is the average professional school. It trains a geographically fixed population in a way no other school attempts. The average seminarian will study for his diocese or province within a seminary system maintained by that diocese or province. Unlike the doctor or lawyer, he will not study in a school and then go off on his own. As a seminarian he is more a prospective member of a family than a prospective professional. The family interrelation ends up taking precedence. Unfortunately, competition among family members often becomes destructive. The official blunting of the student's drive and aggression, the leveling we mentioned above, is as much a recognition that the close quarters of the seminarians' peer relationships cannot tolerate this straightforward competition as it is a desire to keep the beginners in their place.

As the seminarian, following ordination, enters into his life as a priest, these different ways of relating—the official style he learns from the seminary as an institution, the relationships of friendship he develops with chosen friends and counselors, and the complex pattern of peer relationships—all exist side by side. Further, they exist side by side in a relatively nonintegrated way. They are made use of in different situations without notable crossover. One of the tasks of the first year is to integrate these ways of relating.

Focus on Specialization

Another aspect of seminary education that has a blunting effect on the student's pastoral ability is its reliance on specialists. During the course of his studies, the student is exposed to educators who are specialists in their areas of study. They bring an expertise to their work with the students. They have mastered a body of knowledge and now bring that mastery to their students.

Not only is the student exposed to specialists but he is exposed to a broad range of them. Through his years of study he is asked to take courses in philosophy and ethics, in many aspects of both Old and New Testament, as well as courses in moral and dogmatic theology, Church law, Church history, and various aspects of pastoral training. He is asked to spend a number of years in this learning, and in each of the courses the obvious model held up to him is the teacher himself.

Not only does the student pick up the content of the courses but he also learns the methodology that is the foundation for the seminary student's program of instruction. He learns that the ability to demonstrate specialized skills or impart knowledge is the professor's key to membership on the faculty. He also learns, in an equally implicit but still real manner, that the professor's specialized skills and knowledge are the means whereby he relates to the students. Looking at this from a current learning theory, we can say that the medium for the instruction, the seminary itself, is what is principally communicated. And the seminary by itself is a resource for specialized skills and knowledge; it is a model for expertise.

The problem with this model is that the seminarian will not be able to bring the same degree of expertise to all the situations he encounters once he is ordained a priest. Unfortunately, the inability to respond with expertise in each situation is experienced as failure. The seminarian, once ordained, will regard limits to the help he can offer as an admission of defeat. The groundwork for this reaction is laid by the seminary model which relies on and exposes the student to professorial expertise.

The newly ordained priest has much to learn. This reality presents difficulties, not because he is unaware of the need to learn or is unwilling to learn, but because classroom learning is no longer appropriate. And, in large part, he is unfamiliar with other ways of learning which merit his respect and confidence. His seminary years have equipped him with a learning model which works well within the seminary, but much less well in the beginning period of his pastoral work.

Professional Training and Academic Education

In an academic situation what is meant by learning is clear. The same is true in internship training for physicians, or in a school of social welfare. But the model for learning in these situations is different. For the sake of explaining this we can, given the risk of oversimplification, make a distinction between academic and professional learning models. In academic education the prime focus is on ideas. In professional education, there is, additionally, a conscious reflection on the way the student presents himself in the learning situation and his attitudes about that situation. A medical intern who dislikes hospitals is a concern to his preceptors. A graduate student who dislikes universities is not. In addition, in some areas of professional training, as in social welfare, there is a conscious reflection on the learning process itself. Academic education is primarily idea-oriented. There is a transmission of ideas from those who have the knowledge to those who do not, with the expectation that at the end of their period of learning the students will have mastered a body of knowledge in a particular area. In the more experientially oriented professional education there is the expectation that at the end of the learning period the intern will have developed the skills requisite for the practice of his profession. The skills are developed through practice and through evaluative reflection on the quality of his practice.

When the priest begins his work he is in the position of the medical intern or the social worker in training much more than he is in the position of the graduate student. He is called on to relate to people in a way which requires skills as much as it requires a body of knowledge. The difficulty encountered is that frequently he has not had adequate experience with the internship model, the model that allows him to learn skills. He has not had the opportunity to learn those skills which help him relate to people. (As we will point out later, these skills cannot be learned fully prior to ordination because of the important affective response to ordination.) He may have learned about them, but his learning has been more abstract than practical. As a consequence he approaches his work with a handicap. He has been educated following one learning model. He is now called on to enter into a life of ministry, and hopefully this entrance will also be a time of learning. The difficulty here is that for him learning means sitting in class, taking notes, and reading books. Thus he enters his life of ministry with the presupposition that learning is over. The seminary is behind him and now is the time for doing, not for learning. Not having an experiential model at his command he is ill equipped to understand that it is possible to be a learner during this time of doing. As a consequence, this period of learning is not usually put to good advantage.

It might be said, in objection, that seminary courses in field education and summers spent in pastoral ministry have given him this experience. As useful as these are, they fall short of a priestly work experience for several reasons. First, they are short term and involve lower expectations. Second, the seminarian himself usually does not experience the need to make a go of the situation in the way a new priest does. He is learning in a situation he can take or leave, since he will be leaving it in a short while. The priest is learning in a situation in which the judgments on his work, including his own, will stay very much with him. Finally, there is the important and public role that Catholics expect their priests to fulfill, a role they don't expect of the seminarian.

An important task during this first year is instructing the beginning priest in a new model for learning. It is necessary to help him to see that being a fully functioning priest and being a learner are not opposed. This opposition is not merely imaginary, but has been implicitly taught in the seminary course of instruction. One of the benefits to be gained from ordination and from assignment to some pastoral ministry is the freedom from the difficult life of the student. Being subject to the approval and the scrutiny of teachers, being required to master a body of knowledge, having to pass the academic and personal tests which often made his seminary life burdensome; these can now be put behind him. He is ordained, has the faculties of the diocese where he is working, is a fully functioning priest, and no longer need put up with the strictures of student life. He has been preparing for many years, and now he is ready to *do*. To remain a student, to see himself in the student's position, appears to undermine the status of the fully functioning priest which he has worked so long to attain. To be a learner, in effect, means to be a student. And for a long time a prime goal has been to put the life and the status of the student behind him. Learning during this first year of pastoral work requires that this mentality be recognized and that it be dealt with. This can be done effectively only by recognizing the validity of the new priest's desire for status and his need to experience learning in a new and personally useful way.

Influence of Ordination Process

A final point that can be made about the starting point for pastoral work is that it follows upon ordination. The rite of ordination is quite rightly considered to be among the most archetypal of rites. For several months prior to his ordination the average American seminarian is made to feel very special by his fellow seminarians. Should he be working in a parish as a deacon his forthcoming

36

ordination takes on the character of a parish celebration. Progressively, he is singled out and made to feel very special. He is the focal point of a considerable amount of attention. In this, two elements stand out. First, he is progressively being changed from a private person to a public one through conferral of a public role. Second, his own personal part in this is minimal. These two elements come together in the rite of ordination itself. In the ceremony, which is a prime example of a large and public religious celebration combined with impressive rituals, the man who is being ordained is passive. He does nothing, all that is done is done to him. It is only after the completion of the rite proper that he takes on an active role in assisting the bishop during the remainder of the liturgy.

Following the ordination ceremonies, there is a period of celebration and vacation during which time the new priest is publicly presented to and celebrated by his family and home parish, and the fact that he is now a priest is reinforced. When he arrives at his first assignment after this time, he does so with the memory of this celebration very present to him. As we shall see the promise of this period stands out in sharp contrast to realities he encounters.

CHAPTER THREE

models
for entry

Notion of Models

One of the problems with technical sounding titles, such as the title to this chapter, is that we can assume that they apply only in technically well-worked-out situations. To speak of "models for entry" connotes a systematization that is far from the experience of most priests. The very suggestion that a priest was introduced to his work according to a particular model of entry may well elicit responses running from incredulity to black humor. However, as we shall point out, the new priest is in fact introduced to his new situation with ground rules and assumptions at work. His starting out is patterned, and patterned in ways that are common and repeated. Even if the pattern is no more than the repetition of the same neglect, errors, and mistakes over and over again, there is repetition and predictable repetition. This predictable and patterned repetition allows us to speak of models for entry.

A presumption that might be made here is that the different models all have the same goal—the quick and successful entry of the new man into the working situation. The Church and many of its people have invested time and funds in the education of the new priest, and now they are pleased to see this investment come to fruition. The addition of a new priest to a diocesan or religious community is a happy event. We could easily assume that because ordination is such a happy event, and the new priest so welcome, it would be easy for him to get started in his new situation. The opposite usually proves to be true because of several definite problems.

Several questions help surface the problems. What work will he do, and, even more important, whose work will he do? Does this mean easing someone else out of a job? What status is he to have, and what happens if he starts looking better than staff members who are senior to him? How valuable is he to the people with whom he will work? How open is the present staff to anything new, either people or ideas? These questions are answered in the concrete by the reception given him, especially with regard to the specifics of his working situation.

This reception, as noted, is patterned and structured. He is received not only by people but by structures; i.e., not only are there a work superior and co-workers, but they set him to doing things and keep him out of other things in a regular way. He is given jobs to do, given instructions on how to do them and not to do them, and is given or denied tools for his work. In the long run, the structured and depersonalized part of his work can have a much more conditioning effect on the way he fits into his new work than do the people in the situation.

One priest, reflecting on his own first year, commented that he wasn't received in any structured way, that he was left to sink or swim, and learned to swim. This is exactly the point we are making here. This describes the beginning situation of many priests. It happens over and over again with predictable procedures and predictable results. If the patterning of chaos can be seen as a structure, then this is not the absence of a structure, but the presence of one. Were it not for the fact that this proves to be the most common situation we would be tempted to approach it with tongue in cheek. Because it is a reality and because it is common, we will call it the sink-or-swim model. The fact that it is a bad way to assist a new priest into his work does not negate the fact that it is a definable and common way, and thus a model for entry. It is implicit rather than conscious or explicit, and in the concrete appears to happen more by accident than by design, but it is a model nonetheless.

We will examine this model along with several others, moving from the less to the more helpful. These are the sink-or-swim model, which could also be called the laissez-faire model, the military or boot-camp model, the hazing or domesticating model, the apprenticeship model, and the internship model. In addition, we will examine an allied teaching method, which is of notable assistance in helping a newly ordained priest begin his work, the preceptorship model.

It would be a gross oversimplification to suggest that each of these models is a full and distinct way to assist priests in the process of beginning their work, or that they can be clearly graded according to some measure of efficiency. Each does involve, either implicitly or explicitly, a functional attitude toward newcomers. Two of the models, the apprenticeship and internship models, are very conscious attempts at dealing with the process of entry. We will explain all of these models by pinpointing their attitudes toward the beginner and by giving concrete examples of them as they function.

Sink-or-Swim Model

In the sink-or-swim model the initiate is left on his own. He is given minimal assistance, usually some very short instructions at the very beginning, and then is turned loose. This model is not in itself a bad one. It serves quite well in organizations that have a minimal investment in their recruits. Leaflet distributing organizations, door-to-door sales businesses, and the organizations that draw their employees in response to advertisements on matchbooks expect a high turnover in their sales forces. The employees will be given a few minutes of instruction and then turned loose. If they manage to distribute leaflets for a day or two, sell a vacuum cleaner to a supportive relative or some shoes to their neighbors and then give up the whole thing, the employer is not suffering much of a loss. He has placed an absolutely minimal value on the individual employee and expects, even plans for, a very high turnover. It is no accident that companies that use this model frequently employ transients, derelicts, and unstable people.

While this model works well for companies of this sort, it is absolutely destructive within the Church. Few groups, if any, place as high a value on or make as great an investment in the training of their personnel as does the Church. In addition there is the religious dimension of commitment and the importance it has for the Church. This extraordinarily high value should be paralleled by a model for entry which recognizes the value. To make a newly ordained priest and put him in a pastoral situation with a few hours of instructions at the beginning and occasional helpful hints after is as irrational as sending him out to distribute supermarket throwaways. Unfortunately this has been, and remains, a too frequent practice.

The value of this model is not only disproportionate to the value of the personnel it is supposed to be serving, but it is also both ineffective and destructive. It does not help the new priests become integrated into their work situations. It is therefore one of the chief reasons why a number of young clergy leave the priesthood. They never fully become attached to their priestly work because they are not helped to make the attachment. They are set adrift with minimal help at the beginning, and stay adrift. Rather than leave the priesthood they formalize the fact that they have never really entered into it.

There is a common presumption that ordination, of itself, constitutes the process of entry into the priestly life. It does not constitute this process; it begins it. There is a need for an effective follow-up, a supportive process of entry. The sink-or-swim model does not provide this process. It leaves the individual to provide the process by himself and find his own support. A number of priests, unable to do this, remain unattached and at loose ends, both personally and professionally. This state of drifting is too painful to remain unresolved, and the resolutions come in different ways. Some priests, as noted, leave the priesthood. Others move into non-pastoral work which at least gives them a role definition and, in effect, a completion to their process of entry into professional work. Unfortunately, it is entry into work other than that of the priesthood.

Several examples may serve to illustrate the ways in which this state of unattachment is resolved. The first example describes how a priest, left on his own, can be overwhelmed by the sheer difficulty of his work. Father C was assigned to a poor parish with a large transient population, many with alcoholic problems, family problems, and a broad range of the difficulties associated with poverty. The parish also included a small, private hospital. Before he left for his first visit to the hospital he asked the pastor what he should do. The pastor told him to ask for the names of the Catholics and visit them. "Then what do I do?", he asked. "Oh, just do what you can," the pastor replied, which was his stock answer to all such questions. Father C went to the hospital, asked for and received his list, and went to see the first person on it. He entered the room and found an elderly woman in a comatose state. After several minutes of indecision, he administered the last rites and left, not knowing whether or not he had done the right thing.

The second person on the list was a middle-aged man who was watching television from his bed. Father C entered and introduced himself. The man turned, looked at Father C over his glasses, said nothing, and turned back to the television set. After a few minutes of mounting anxiety, Father C blurted, "Well, I've got to be going," and left.

With the final courage remaining he went to the next person on his list, an older woman undergoing treatment for cancer. She was very relieved to see Father C, informed him she was divorced and remarried, hadn't been to confession for twenty-eight years, and wanted him to hear her confession. Aware that according to Church law the woman was in an irregular situation, yet wanting to be compassionate, he did not know what to do. He had heard his first confession only two weeks previously. Father C made a few very confused comments about difficult situations, heard her confession, and left feeling both inadequate and compromised. As he walked home, he realized further that he had been more concerned about the legality of his own actions than about her and her illness, a realization that deepened his sense of failure. Ever after, he approached visits to the hospital with dread, and made them as infrequently as possible.

His preaching, counseling, and pastoral work in general impressed him as being equally ineffectual, for the poor were still poor and the alcoholics still stumbling on the street in front of the church. He could see no success in his efforts because he had no gauge for measuring success, and there was no one to help him see that his efforts were good. Each day presented him with new tasks he felt unable to accomplish. After six months of pastoral work he felt no more accomplished than he did at the beginning, primarily because there was no one to help him understand what constituted an accomplishment in working with such troubled people. A year later, after his sense of personal failure, frustration, and disappointment had grown to an unbearable state, he left the priesthood. To add to his injury, his departure was almost as unnoticed officially as were his pastoral efforts.

Another issue which complicates the already difficult sink-or-swim situation is the qualified welcome extended to a new man. Some priests may be left on their own quite simply because their pastors or work superiors do not know what else to do. Others may be left on their own because the new superior is not that happy at having a new man on his staff. Father A was assigned to a large parish following ordination. The pastor, a vocal man with strong views, did not like the changes in the Church and saw Father A as a product of what he disliked. As a consequence, Father A was very rarely scheduled to preach at any Mass and was never scheduled to take a turn at preaching at all the Sunday Masses, as was the practice in the parish. The pastor, from the pulpit, would make disparaging comments about "these young priests," and frequently criticized Father A for not knowing what he was doing. At first hurt and angered by this treatment, Father A moved progressively to a state of bewilderment verging on panic. His best efforts were continually disparaged by the pastor. Given no yardstick, other than the pastor's negative judgments, against which to measure his accomplishments, and being intelligent enough to see that he had, indeed, made some mistakes, he moved into a crisis of serious self-doubt and vocational uncertainty. The pastor's comments that Father A's ordination was a mistake raised the question in his own mind. He resolved the question by leaving the priesthood.

There was nothing particularly wrong with Father A's work. Indeed, he did much good work. The problem was that he was assigned to a parish where he was not welcome. He needed direction and was given none. The pastor did not want him or any young priest in his parish. He made his feelings felt, and he succeeded in getting rid of him.

In the following two examples, each priest was assigned to a difficult situation with no structured support. Each of them was competent and intelligent, and each had a very real desire to do well. But they were left on their own to cope with the demands of the ministry, and given no criteria to understand what doing well meant in their particular situations. This proved to be more than they could handle. Each left the priesthood in an unofficial way for work in a more supportive context.

Father D, after a year working in an inner-city parish, decided that he needed professional training to learn how to cope with pastoral work with a degree of competence. He entered a two-year program in social work. The social work program was designed to help its trainees deal with the difficulties encountered in helping troubled people. It gave them an intellectual understanding of emotional and social upset. It helped them recognize their own anxieties in these situations and to see that these anxieties did not bespeak any inabilities on their part. Father D was given an appreciation for his own strengths as manifested in his work. The group of trainees in the program provided a support for this learning.

Father D found this program the most helpful support he had received up to that point. It provided him with answers to many questions raised during the course of his pastoral work. Because of his positive experience, he decided to become a social worker. He stayed within the context of the priesthood but abandoned all intentions of a pastoral ministry for the specialized work of the social worker.

Father E, who had great hopes for working with people, requested and received permission to return to school after a year and a half in a poor parish with a kind but rather reclusive pastor. His work was good but he was unable on his own to come up with a way to put limits on the demands placed on his time and energies without feeling terribly guilty. He felt drained, no longer able to meet the needs of his parishioners and saw no way out of his situation other than to leave it behind him. He entered a program in library science and became a librarian in a Catholic college. Here, pastoral ministry was left behind in favor of a work that presented him with very few personal contacts. While he was officially still a priest in good standing, his ministry was limited to occasional Masses and confessions for the religious who maintained the college.

In these examples, the beginning priests were left to sink or swim, and they all sank, each in a different way. Frequently this is seen as a judgment of the priest in question—in my opinion, mistakenly so. It is more appropriately seen as a judgment on the foolishness of turning a man loose in a demanding and difficult situation with no real support, no direction, and no usable standards for judging effectiveness and ineffectiveness in work, and then expecting him to develop that sense of competence necessary to survive. Support, reward, protection, and recognition are necessary in any long-term working situation. To deprive the beginning priest of these, as the sink-or-swim model does, is to set him up for failure.

Military Model

The military model is a much more structured and involved model than the sink-or-swim model. It recognizes the need to give the newcomer attention and time. The name is drawn from the common practice in the military of having a period of basic training or boot camp. The recruits are given a period of initiation and training which is explicit and direct, and which very much recognizes their need to become attached. It is unpleasant, usually involves a considerable amount of browbeating, and seeks to help the new man become part of the organization by substituting a common *persona* for his own personality.

The military model has two goals, in addition to helping the man become attached to his new organization. The first is to instill a sense of obedience. The second is to teach him how to operate under crisis conditions. The model was common in the Church a generation ago. Many older priests looked on their first pastor much in the way a new recruit looks on his drill instructor—with fear and apprehension. It was effective in training obedient priests who could be counted on to do what they were told to do. However, because of the stress it created, it stifled the development of an ability to respond creatively to crisis situations. This model is no longer common in the Church, in large part because the attitude toward authority no longer permits a pastor to get away with acting like a drill sergeant or martinet.

Domesticating Model

A model which is somewhat like the boot camp model and which is still common is the domesticating model. Like the boot camp model, it is authoritarian, but it is more oriented to teaching a new man how to fit into the system than to elicit instant obedience. In the domesticating model the new man is taught how not to rock the boat, how to keep a low profile, and how to postpone his own gratification. Within this model the newcomer is given a number of tasks and assignments that both keep him busy and teach him that he is the most junior of staff members. He will often be given low status work, such as early morning Masses, emergency nighttime calls at the hospital, and assignments that notably cut into his comfort. In addition, he will often be given the jobs that no one else wants, such as the chaplaincy of parish groups that are particularly uninteresting, or work with parishioners with a very low status, such as the altar boys. He is made to feel very much the low man on the staff, as the following example illustrates.

Father G reported that his reception in the rectory made him feel like an outsider. He noted that on the most recent Sunday, at dinner after the last Mass, he was seated on a kitchen chair because the last dining room chair was offered to a guest. In the table conversation, no effort was made to include him. Finally, although it was not his day to be on duty, he was told that he should stay in the rectory and cover for emergency calls since the other priests were all going away for the afternoon.

Father G was both angered and offended by this treatment. What he did not quite grasp was that this was not just inadvertent bad manners. It came from a belief on the part of the older priests that this sort of treatment is good for the new priest. Often the older priests would speak of the need to "keep them humble." It was their belief that hazing and ego-deflating were appropriate responses for a newcomer.

A second incident, illustrating another side of this model, shows that the newcomer is often hazed as a means for keeping him from threatening the status and security of the permanent staff members. Underlying this treatment is the fear that the newcomer might in fact succeed in a way that could lead to the replacement of the older staff.

Father K had been given charge of three parish groups: the altar society, the children's religion classes, and the publication of the weekly newsletter. These were considered burdensome and low-status responsibilities. After meeting initially with the first two groups and the individuals who took charge of the newsletter, he applied himself to the work creatively. He started a series of pastoral visits to the homes of the elderly members of the Altar Society, and responded quite sensitively to a number of the issues of aging. He was able to shift the religion classes from a purely content-oriented to an issue-oriented program, and increased the number of students who came to its sessions. He also began including more items of parish interest in the newsletter and made it more visually attractive.

These successes of his were not greeted with applause within the rectory. He was told to check with the pastor before making any home visits, to go back to the strictly content-oriented religion program, and to put the writing of the newsletter in the hands of the parish secretary. As it turned out he was receiving too much gratification for the work he was doing, and within a system which presupposed, albeit implicitly, that junior staff members are to receive gratification.

The issues at stake were the questions of his status and the quality of his welcome. Father K was welcome provided that he did not threaten any of the senior staff. His competence and charm were a threat. Success could lead to a higher visibility than that offered by the other men on the staff, and this higher visibility would bring with it a change in status. He was expected to maintain a low status, a low profile, assist the older men in their work, support them in their higher status, status that they had worked for years to attain, and seek his own gratification at a future time.

Father K perceived this message correctly. He noted that "they're really trying to put me down." His difficulty was believing that it was really happening—then living with it. He had difficulty reconciling the support and visibility that he had been given at the time of his ordination with the low status given to him a few short weeks later. When he was helped to see that his welcome was, in fact, a qualified one, and that the qualification centered around the question of status, he resented what he considered the small-mindedness of his confreres. Nonetheless, understanding the situation, he was able to cope with it. Initially he was bewildered by the chilly reception his pastoral efforts were met with in the rectory. He began to question his effectiveness, and was beset by self-doubt. When he was helped (by his preceptor, or supervisor) to understand the situation, his feelings of bewilderment and self-doubt were replaced by feelings of anger at this particular system and at the senior staff. But as irksome as this was, the feelings were appropriate, focused, and could be coped with.

Father K was not left at loose ends when he arrived in the parish, nor in any sense set adrift. Very definite expectations were made of him, and what was expected was that he work at jobs that were not personally rewarding nor helpful in ingratiating him with the people. He had to go through a period of hazing before he could be considered as having earned the right to these privileges. As one of the senior staff members put it, "After you've proved yourself around here, you'll find it's a very nice place to be." An essential part of the proof was the demonstration of the fact that he was not out to replace the senior staff, nor take away any of their status or privilege.

Another aspect of the domesticating or hazing model is the belief that this sort of hazing process is positively helpful and morally strengthening. This attitude is not limited to clergy. It is analogous to one aspect of the training given to medical students until recently. Oftentimes they were required to do menial tasks, such as scrubbing floors, in the belief that this sort of humbling work would be useful in making them into disciplined and service-oriented doctors.

Apprenticeship Model

The next model we will examine is the apprenticeship model. In this model the new man is, in effect, apprenticed to an older priest who teaches him how to go about priestly work by involving him in his own work. It recognizes the new man's need for introduction, his need for information about his setting, his need to know people, and for support in his work. It's chief drawback is that it is time-consuming and demands a lot of the older man, but if he is willing and able to provide the instruction, it usually proves helpful, as the following example illustrates.

Father F was assigned to a parish in a town with a large Catholic population. The pastor, an older man who was well-known in the town, took Father F in tow as he went about his work. First, he drove him around town and pointed out the stores and services he would need to know about. He introduced Father F to the people he might have to contact in the course of his work so that he would already have a relationship with them—town officials, people in charge of the public welfare offices, doctors, nurses in the hospital emergency room, the town undertaker. He also introduced Father F to the more active people in the parish and, at all of the Masses on one Sunday, introduced him to the parish. He commented on his sermons, gave him suggestions about counseling people, and, prior to his first funeral, wedding and baptism, showed him how to go about each ceremony.

Father F found this quite helpful. When emergencies arose he knew where to turn. In his regular work he had a sense of being supported and had the feeling that the pastor was glad to have him on the staff. The only drawback, a minor one, was that being taken around to meet all these people made him feel very much the beginner and seemed a little demeaning.

Recognizing the ease with which this model can be implemented, we may well wonder why it is not more commonly used. The answer to this question is to be found not in the model itself but in the quality of the human relationships found in the rectory. Living and working together in the same place requires a type of relationship that does not foster the apprenticeship model. Why this is so will be explained in our final chapter.

Internship Model

The last model we will examine is the internship model. Internship as a learning model is drawn largely from medical training. The intern has finished his formal education, is granted his professional title, and is given fully responsible work to do. He is responsible for the quality of his work, and yet is seen as a professional who is still in the learning process. The presupposition that he is still a learner and that the hospital staff will help him with his learning is built right into the system.

This model proves both possible and useful for beginning priests, as the situation of Father R illustrates. Father R was assigned to a large city parish in an area that was changing from middle class German, Irish, and Italian families to Afro-American and Spanish-speaking families. Prior to his assignment to the parish, the areas of his responsibilities were spelled out in considerable detail. The parish had been subdivided into several areas with a staff member responsible for each area, and he was assigned to one. It was decided that it would be the geographic area with people from the socio-economic group most similar to his own in order to make the transition less difficult. Within his geographic area he was asked to spend about one third of his time working with families in preparing children for the Sacraments of Baptism, First Communion, and Confirmation. He was asked to meet with couples preparing for marriage in order to discuss the theology of marriage with them. In addition, with reference to what the pastor called the "feeling-tone" of the parish, he articulated for Father R that "we want to see the clergy working with the people and meeting their religious needs, not trying to fit them into a preconceived notion of what church obligations are." Father R and the pastor also clarified the fact that he was there for just one year with beginning and ending dates clearly stated. They agreed on the work he was expected to do and established objective standards for what the pastor considered acceptable and unacceptable work.

During the course of the year the pastor was able to help Father R see his strengths, and to articulate for him why his good work was good. He also helped him see his weak areas, and worked with him both to see that the weak areas were covered by other members of the staff and to teach him how to go about compensating for his weaknesses. Both his praise and criticisms were made concrete with examples Father R was able to grasp easily.

In this example of the internship model, the conscious and direct effort by the pastor to teach the newcomer how to go about and evaluate his work proved to be effective. He helped Father R understand why some work was good and why some was less productive. He was also able to help him see how he presented himself, how other people saw him, and what his strengths and weaknesses were. In addition, he spelled out very clear responsibilities for the beginning priest. Where these were fulfilled well Father R was given public recognition, and where the work was done less well, he was informed quietly, avoiding public criticism, and was advised constructively with a possible remedy. Father R experienced this process as very supportive rather than burdensome, and was quick to point out that this support was a major factor in helping him over the difficult areas as he started out.

It is obvious that Father R was fortunate in having this pastor as he began his priestly work. However, it should be noted that the pastor was primarily a pastor, not a teacher. His chief concern was the quality of the work done by the parish staff, not Father R's learning. Father R attended the weekly staff meetings, and all instruction took place during these meetings, which lasted no more than two hours each week.

The pastor's efforts at instructing Father R, while uncommon, were not idiosyncratic. He utilized an instructional method that is common in other professions, and did so in a typical parish. His ability to provide for Father R's informational and support needs, which will be described in the next chapter, is not an extraordinary ability. What is extraordinary is that this method, which works so well and is common in other professions, is utilized so little. The reason why it worked in this situation may lie in the fact that Father R and the pastor did not share the same living situation. He did not live in the rectory and thus shared only a working relationship with the pastor. As we noted above with the apprenticeship model, combining living and working relationships presents special problems, problems which we will explain in the last chapter.

Preceptorship Model of Learning

Each of these models for entry describes a way to introduce a newcomer into his work. The preceptorship model, which we will now describe, differs from these models both in goals and method. The goal in the preceptorship model is to provide a means to help the new man make sense of, learn from, and ultimately cope with the issues that arise during the process of entry. It does so by providing the individual with a teacher, a preceptor, who will help him with these issues. We can understand this better if we contrast what takes place in the preceptorship situation with what happens in the entry models.

In each of the entry models, the work superior is usually responsible for the quality of the work the newcomer performs. If he is a pastor, he will want the new man to do a good job, for he has a serious obligation to see that his people are well served. The preceptor, on the other hand, is not responsible for the outcome of the work. He does not have to demand success or excellence. He can help the beginner learn from his mistakes just as easily as he can help him learn from his successes. The pastor cannot do this; he wants good work. The difference here is the difference between an employer and a teacher. The one wants good work, the other wants learning. The pastor or work superior has a necessary connection with the work; the preceptor may well have no contact with the work situation, only with the beginning priest. The work superior focuses on the work, the preceptor on the relationship between the new man and his work. This model is frequently called the supervisory model, and the teacher a supervisor. We are not using it here only to avoid confusion with the countless work situations where the supervisor is a work superior and responsible for the quality of the employee's work.

It is possible for the preceptorship model to work in conjunction with the preceding models. This is becoming a more common situation in the Church. In the deacon-training programs operated by diocesan seminaries, there is usually a faculty member whose goal is to help the deacons reflect on their work. They are not responsible for the quality of the student's work. That is the role of the pastor. Rather, they are concerned with the student's learning. The pastoral training programs for priests and religious, as well as those which are common in the Protestant tradition, make use of this model. It is frequently within the context of preceptorship relationships that the more fundamental issues of entry surface. it is helpful to have this preceptorship situation because the entry models, with their focus on pastoral work and the integration of the newcomer into the working situation, do not foster the reflective and subjective context which promotes a surfacing of the entry issues.

This preceptorship relationship can be established with equal usefulness on a less formal basis between priests and a trained professional in their area of concern. It is becoming more common for priests to arrange for regular meetings with consultants in which they can discuss the priest's agenda. These sessions, focusing as they do on the relationship between the priest and his work, can be of considerable help in assisting the priest to understand and firm up that relationship.

An added plus in a good preceptorship relationship is the model that is demonstrated. Not only does the priest receive help, but he has a firsthand experience of a good, helpful teacher at work. Within this preceptorship relationship he learns not only how to cope with issues as they arise but he is given an example of a way of helping people. This modeling can often be as useful as the content of the discussions themselves.

Several times we have mentioned the issues that come up during the period of entry. There are several of these and they prove to be as significant as they are common. We will go on to examine these in the next section.

CHAPTER 4

the first year's agenda

Three Major Tasks

In the preceding chapters we have illustrated several crisis situations that developed as new priests began their work. As he starts out, the new man is faced with a number of important issues that can become crises. Of their nature, however, these are not crisis issues. They are more properly seen as tasks in need of accomplishing. Their accomplishment is necessary for a successful entry into pastoral work. It is when these tasks are not accomplished that crises arise. We will single out and look at three of these tasks in some detail.

The first is the need for the new priest to become an integral part of the pastoral setting where he will work. He has been ordained and given a public role as a Church official. Also, he has been given an assignment with the duties, rights, and privileges that go with the assignment. But, he is still a stranger to that pastoral setting. He is an outsider, and it will take effort and assistance before he becomes a part of it. The process of becoming an insider is a task we will call affiliation.

A second task is the need to learn how to define the work he is to do. Perhaps the most common source of failure in the work done by clergy is that the help sought of them and the help they offer do not mesh. Many of the clergy's best efforts, while generous and well-intentioned, miss the mark. A prime task, then, is developing an analytic ability which will help him understand what is being sought of him and what he has to offer, when the two do and do not mesh, and finally how to handle situations when they do not. This analytic ability we will call contracting. Learning how to contract is one of the new priest's prime tasks.

The third task is the completion of the process of specifying his self-view as a pastor. This process was begun with the priest's first pastoral experiences in the seminary or elsewhere and with his reactions to these experiences. In the pattern of likes and dislikes that begins to emerge from his work we can find the beginnings of a pastoral orientation. Now as he begins his priestly work many options lie open before him. Many expectations will be placed on him. Often these expectations are a function of the roles traditional to the priesthood. Articulating these roles, deciding which expectations he can meet and which he cannot meet, and learning how to cope with both the roles and the expectations will prove a major challenge. In the process of meeting this challenge he should be accomplishing the task of foregoing his priestly or pastoral identity in a way which will allow him to work in a personally satisfying and effective manner. This task we will call the establishment of pastoral identity. We will examine each of these three tasks in turn.

Affiliation

The first task we will look at is affiliation, the need to become an insider. The new priest has been given an assignment, but this does not mean that he automatically becomes an insider in his new job. This is a difficult process. It requires time and assistance. When he approaches his new work situation he is an outsider and needs help in becoming an insider.

The fact of ordination often belies this reality. It often seems as though by the very fact of being ordained he should be an insider. He is a priest, but that is not the same as having living and working relationships in his new assignment. These have to be worked out. In many ways the complex of human relationships that is to be found in any pastoral setting is its most significant element. These relationships have to be established through risk and effort.

One of the difficulties in becoming an insider is that it depends in large part on the good will, sensitivity, and intelligence of those who are already insiders. If they help the new priest become part of the organization then his chances of making it are notably increased. If they block him, either consciously or unconsciously, there is a very good probability that he will not make it. The insider, be he a priest or another staff member who has been around for a while and who feels at home in the setting, has an advantage over the outsider. His willingness or unwillingness to share his advantage can notably affect the new man's situation, as the following examples illustrate. The first illustrates how the beginning priest can be shown up as a newcomer, and how disadvantageous this position can be.

Father W, newly assigned to a campus ministry, arrived for a committee meeting. He had been assigned this committee as his responsibility and was expected to chair the meeting. The outgoing chairman, an older staff member of the campus ministry, had agreed to introduce him and get things started. However, the older priest did not show up and, feeling the pressure of time and the growing nervousness of the students, Father W decided to begin. He had a hard time getting things going because he did not know the committee members, nor they him. About one half hour after the meeting started, the old staff member arrived, greeted the committee members whom he knew rather warmly and then sat back with the question, "Well, what have you been doing?" Father W briefly recapitulated the meeting. The older priest asked, "Oh, you haven't done thus and such?", and then went on to outline succinctly what should have been done. Father W felt quite embarrassed at this point, his newcomer's shortcomings painfully evident.

The older staff member, either consciously or unconsciously, had set him up for this. He allowed him to begin unaided, to make the mistakes a beginner would make, and then came in and publicly pointed them out. The older man was the insider, he knew both the people and the right thing to do, and as such he had an advantage. For whatever reason he was unwilling to share this advantage with the new man. Father W's disadvantaged position as an outsider was made even weaker and more disadvantaged as a result of the meeting. Relative to his task of becoming part of the pastoral setting, he ended up in a worse position afer the meeting than he was in before it began.

The situation of Father C offers a contrast. When he arrived at his first assignment the pastor welcomed him publicly and warmly at all the Masses on a given Sunday. He drove him around and introduced him to the prominent people in the town as his new assistant. He introduced him to the staff of a public institution which was in the parish and whose care fell to the parish, and he introduced him to those people in the parish whose assistance and volunteer efforts were integral parts of the parish's survival. In effect, he was bringing in Father C with a stamp of approval and in a supportive way.

Accompanying this willingness to help Father C get started was the reality that this willingness to help is often accompanied by some hard bargaining. Father C was given the early Masses, some of the more demanding and less gratifying parish work, and the responsibility for the night calls from the hospital. In effect, the pastor was saying that he had the opportunity to become an insider, but he was going to have to work for it. He was going to have to prove himself by doing well in the less prestigious and more menial jobs on a parish staff. Nonetheless, he was assured that he was welcome and the people knew of his welcome, that the means for becoming an insider were given to him, and that the price he would have to pay was spelled out. His process of affiliation was off to a good start.

As he begins the move from the outside to becoming an insider in his pastoral work the new priest is faced with several areas of need. If these needs are not met, his affiliation into his new work can be seriously hampered. We will examine these needs under three different headings. While this division proves useful we do not suggest that it is the only possible one. The areas are informational needs, physical needs, and emotional needs.

Prime among the informational needs is the need for an overview of his new organization. Goals, responsibilities, territorial limits, finances, and personnel are all important factors, and the new man must know about each of these. This might seem sufficiently obvious that it could be taken for granted. However, it is common for the new man to be uninformed about some important areas of his new work setting. In the process of getting to work and of meeting the needs that come up as soon as he arrives, the task of informing him adequately about his new situation can get sidetracked. It is only later on, often under the pressure of the moment, that he discovers that he doesn't know where certain streets are, or how to get to a local hospital in an emergency, or who assigns the lectors or ushers for the Sunday liturgy, or where the parish's financial records are kept, or who has the keys to all the locked doors.

In addition to the overview of his new setting the new man needs to know the chain of command and what his setting's organizational chart looks like. Further, he needs to know not only the theoretical chain of command, but the real one as well, for the two rarely coincide. Part of this is the discovery of those people who are key people for him in his work, regardless of whether or not they would appear as key on an organizational chart. The following examples can serve to illustrate these organizational questions.

Father D began his work as a hospital chaplain. He was assigned responsibility for several floors in a large hospital. The director introduced him to the head nurse on each floor who, in turn, introduced him to the other nurses, nursing assistants, and the interns and residents who worked on his floor. He took these introductions seriously, for he saw all these people as colleagues and wanted to maintain good personal and working relationships with each of them. He also believed that once these introductions were over, he had come to know the key people in his area of responsibility.

Father D had been taught by a hospital chaplain that it was appropriate and often helpful to prepare relatives for the death of a patient. Further, the chaplain had told him that this should be done a few hours before death in order to allow the family time to adjust to the fact, but not so far in advance that they would go through many hours of anxious waiting. One elderly patient seemed gravely ill and Father D wanted to find out whether she was in danger of death. He asked the head nurse who hesitated and then said that that information should come from the doctor. He went to the doctor and asked him whether or not the elderly patient was going to die. The doctor replied that the patient was seriously ill, that chances of recovery seemed minimal, but that they were doing all they could. Father D picked up the doctor's defensiveness and felt frustrated. He had no desire of questioning the care the patient was receiving. All he wanted to know was whether he should be prepared to say the prayers for the dying.

At this point one of the housekeeping staff, a woman who cleaned the patient's rooms and to whom Father D had been polite and kind, but with whom he had never spoken at any length, beckoned to him and said that she wished to speak to him. She told him that the elderly patient probably would not last more than a few more hours, and that it might be good for him to tell this to the family. She added that sometimes when the priest said the prayers for the dying, some of the relatives who felt up to it could be there with him and assist in the prayers. She also said that it was often more helpful to give this information to the families in the solarium at the end of the hall, which happened right now to be empty, rather than to tell them this in the hallway. Father D thanked her and then asked the relatives to come into the solarium. As they gathered around a small table the woman appeared out of nowhere and unobtrusively put a tray with a pot of tea, cups, and cookies on the table and slipped out quietly. He helped the family to tea, and as they drank their tea he told them that it seemed that the end might be near, that he was going to say the prayers for the dying and that, if they liked, they could be with him in the room and, if they chose, assist him in this. They did wish to accompany him and shortly after they finished the patient died.

Father D was quick to see that he had a very strong ally and support in his work in this insignificant member of the housekeeping staff. He also came to see that some information that he needed in his work, information about the emotional state of patients, as well as their physical condition, could be given to him more easily by the housekeeping staff who were in and out of the patients' rooms all day, than by the medical staff. The housekeeping staff, who appeared at the very bottom of the organizational chart, were very key people to him in his work. Some of those who appeared at the top of the organizational chart, like the chief of staff and the medical director, he saw very infrequently. We can anticipate that in any organization some of the key people will appear on the organizational chart and some will not. The organizational chart is not an accurate representation of authority. The beginning priest, as he tries to move into his pastoral setting, needs to know not only who the official key people are but, in addition, who are the less visible and unofficial key people.

Another example of this can be found in the situation of Father A. Assigned to a parish, he quickly learned that an individual, very low on the organizational chart, could be very significant to his work, but in a negative way. The organizational chart would have shown the significant people to be the pastor, two assistants, the principal of the school, the president of the parish council, and the head of the parochial school board. In addition, there were the teachers in the school and the heads of the other parish organizations. There was also a retired man who worked as a general handyman and janitor. He unlocked the church in the morning and locked it at night, did the same with the school, repaired any broken windows or faulty locks, and directed the efforts of a group of volunteers in washing and waxing floors wherever and whenever this was needed. Further, he volunteered his services. He also kept all the keys. For some reason which he never understood, Father A ran afoul of him from the very beginning. The results were horrendous. The church somehow did not get unlocked on the mornings that he was to say Mass. The school was locked up when he tried to meet there with the parochial school board. Father A always had to see to it that he had a cruet with wine in it stashed away in the rectory refrigerator because it often turned out right before his Mass that there was no wine around. In similar ways, he discovered that this officially insignificant person who also had all the keys was quite literally a key person.

Father A presented his problem to the pastor who recognized what was going on. The pastor, hard pressed to meet the ever growing expenses of the parish school sympathized with him and told him that they could always replace this man with a paid janitor and go that much deeper into debt. Father A added that it would probably be simpler in the long run to get a new assistant, and the pastor agreed. Putting their heads together they decided to win over the janitor through public thanks and praise. Father A preached a sermon on Christian generosity and used the janitor's donated services to the parish as his example of what his could mean in the concrete. The man was both surprised and pleased, and the problem ended as quickly as it began.

It would be possible to conclude with the simple statement that there are a lot of important people who don't appear on organizational charts. While this is true it does not recognize the very special circumstances at work in a Catholic institution. To begin with, the clergy are accustomed to equate sacramental authority with administrative authority. The beginning priest, trained to value and lead the Church's sacramental life, can be expected to underestimate the importance of unordained administrators. Most parish organizational charts would list the assistant pastor in a position superior to that of the parish secretary. In fact, in many parishes the parish secretary is often the number two person in importance in the running of the parish after the pastor. In a parallel structure in the business world, she would probably be listed as in an executive position. In many parishes contacts between clergy and laity go through her filter. She decides which requests stay in her hands and which ones go to the clergy. But because of the special sacral role of the priests the significance of lay employees and staff is frequently underestimated.

In addition, there is the very special fact that the rectory is not only a place of business but a home for the clergy. This makes for a very definite set of problems which we will discuss later. At this point we can note that those people who play a significant role in the rectory as home, namely, the housekeeper and/or cook, have an importance out of proportion to their relation to the work of the parish. As the beginning priest enters his pastoral work these individuals, significant in the rectory, can be a major source of help or hindrance to him in his Church work, although they have no direct connection with it and would not be listed on the Church's organizational chart.

In addition to the key people in any organization there is also a chain of command. As with the question of key people there is both a theoretical and a real chain of command. It is common for beginning priests to underestimate the degree to which they are accountable to the laity. The average chain of command will have the priest accountable to the pastor and bishop and, in some parishes, the parish council. Many a priest has discovered to his chagrin that there are individuals in his parish to whom he is accountable because of their insistence on an accounting. They can make this insistence felt through critical letters written to the bishop, through stirring up public opposition to him, or through a more covert undermining of his competence and authority. As he begins his work, he would be well advised to find out the people to whom he must render an account, and either give them their accounting or a rationale why he will not.

Places can be as primary as people. It is important for the beginning priest to know where work is done as it is to know who does the work. Further, it is quite possible that the place where the work gets done proves to be a different place from where it would appear to be in theory. One priest reported that it took him six months to discover that the real decisions in the parish were made not at the

63

parish council meeting but at the informal coffee session following one of the Sunday Masses. At that time the pastor would circulate and, sounding out key people in the parish, make plans and decisions. The parish council, which the new priest attended and to whom he looked for decision-making, did no more than rubber-stamp the Sunday morning proposals. This was not because of some deviousness on the part of the pastor or people, but rather was due to the fact that they were much more able to use a family model of decision-making than they were an organizational model. They felt quite comfortable deciding things over coffee, but felt quite out-of-place and unable to function while sitting around a committee room table.

The second of the three areas of need mentioned above is the area of physical needs. This refers, quite simply, to the space and tools necessary for work. The difficulty faced by the beginning priest is that the expectations placed on him, both by his people and by himself, often require more in the way of physical resources than he has at his disposal. The lack of these resources may be due to insufficient funds, it may be due to a more limited view of the ministry on the part of the superiors, or it may be part of an attempt to restrain the new man until he proves himself. No matter what the cause, the result, a hampering of the new man, is common.

The physical needs can include such things as an office or place to work, an automobile, money, a telephone, and access to secretarial help. It is not uncommon for one or several of these to be lacking. When there are a limited number of parlors or offices and their use must be scheduled it is not uncommon for the most junior of assistants to lose out when the scheduling results in conflict. When he is assigned a project, or a group to work with, again it is common for the new priest to have inadequate funds. Frequently, he will underestimate his expenses either as a way of pleasing the pastor or of economizing. This can lead to curtailing his program.

The following brief incidents illustrate examples of the problems caused by shortages in the area of basic tools for work. One priest reported that the rectory had only three telephones. One was in the pastor's bedroom, one was in the kitchen, and the other was in the parish office. As a result he could neither receive nor make telephone calls with any privacy. This hampered his work. Another priest was assigned responsibility for the parish teenage group. Together they planned for several winter skiing trips. A shortage of funds and the pastor's unwillingness within the financially hard-pressed parish to sacrifice for what he considered purely recreational programs caused them to be cancelled. The beginning priest's standing in the eyes of the people, and in his own eyes, fell.

A third priest had the responsibility for duplicating the lesson forms and readings used by the teachers in religious education. The duplicating machine was in the pastor's office. In order to run off the material he had to spend several hours each week working in the pastor's office. In order not to intrude he found himself arranging his own time in order to work there when the pastor was absent. Even so, he felt like an intruder and was apologetic about the time spent in the pastor's office.

Each of these examples involved a situation in which the basic tools needed for his assigned work were either unavailable or available only with difficulty. To assign a task to a man and then deny him the means to accomplish that task is both unreasonable and bad organizational practice. What proves significantly typical is that the priests accepted the unreasonableness of their respective situations as a given. The first priest could have insisted on his own telephone. The second could have insisted on the funds necessary for the work. The third, that the duplicating machine be put in an accessible and public place. This did not happen. They each saw the unreasonableness of the situation, but acquiesced before their own sense of frustration and failure. This sense of failure, coming at the beginning of pastoral work, is especially destructive. Failure or minimal achievement in assigned or self-established goals work to keep the beginner an outsider. One of the prime questions he has as he enters the working situation, "Can I make it in this work?" is being answered negatively. His ability to take chances, which he must do if he is to succeed in his work, will be diminished by these negative experiences, and his learning will be affected adversely.

This brings us to the third of the three areas of need, the area of emotional needs. Support, guidance, gratification, protection, and a feeling of competence are very real needs, and if they are not met, the new man may experience a painful and incomplete entry into pastoral work.

The beginning priest needs support. He needs to know that his new superior and colleagues wish to see him succeed, that they are on his side and see his success as a positive achievement for all of them. Earlier, we cited the case of Father K whose success in his pastoral work was not received positively by his fellow staff members. This type of reception is unfortunate because the new man is in a particularly vulnerable position. He has no reservoir of success on which he can draw for his own support. Being helped to do well, having his success indicated, and being given all the tools necessary to do well are areas of support on which he should be able to count.

One area of support that is troublesome is the extent of his reliance on volunteer help. Frequently, the beginning priest is given the responsibility for achieving goals which depend largely on the goodwill and donated services of volunteers. Father M, in his first assignment, was given charge of the liturgy for the folk Mass and responsibility for the altar boys. In each case he was dealing with people whose presence was very visible and very important. Their absence was also noted, for they had specific functions to perform before a church full of people. Further, they looked on the contribution of their services as a favor to Father M, and in no way felt obligated to show up for their work on a regular basis. He reported that he was becoming an expert in the art of bribing twelve-year-olds, but was having more difficulty in finding the right price for the adolescents in the folk group.

His position was made more difficult in that the other priests considered it his responsibility to make sure that the altar boys and the folk musicians showed up for their work. It would have been more appropriate, and probably more effective, to look at the need to assure the presence of the altar boys and the musicians for the folk Mass as a parish responsibility, and one which fell on the clergy in the order of their authority in the parish. Father M, as the newest and youngest member of the staff, had the least amount of leverage in working with volunteers in a situation where leverage was important. Thus, he went into a situation in which there was a high possibility of failure. The support he needed was not present. While the presence of altar boys and folk musicians might not be major in the overall work of the Church, they were major responsibilities for Father M, and areas in which he could prove his ability to work as an effective part of the parish staff. In his beginning work his chances for success were notably diminished.

In addition, the beginning priest has a need for guidance. Father P, several months into his new work, was sought out by a young woman, a mother of three, who was separated from her husband. The woman was a dependent individual and was also rather manipulative. Within a short time, through appeals to his generosity, she had maneuvered Father P into a position in which he was spending a lot of time and energy listening to her, running errands, and, in general, making up for the lack of emotional support and stability caused by the departure of her husband. He felt uncomfortable in this position but also saw no way out.

His pastor, recognizing what was going on, pointed out to him that there was an alternative between becoming a substitute husband or closing the door to the woman's very real needs. He helped Father P to see that the woman was going to have to learn to become more self-reliant and independent, and learn how to find emotional supports without turning people off by her incessant demands on them. He also agreed to direct his efforts in teaching the young woman how to learn these lessons, and in the course of a year Father P helped her strengthen her abilities to cope in a more self-directed manner. In this case the pastor not only provided Father P with guidance but also showed him, by example, what good guidance could do.

Protection is also a very real need. The new man needs to know that if major criticisms start to come his way that he will be protected. He needs to know that there is someone who will go to bat for him in times of trouble. He needs to know that his own personal weaknesses will not be allowed to overwhelm him or render him ineffective in his work or unhappy in his personal life.

The need for protection is more important than is commonly recognized. The new priest will occasionally have to take unpopular stands or choose sides in struggles. When he does so he may find a lot of anger and criticism directed at him. He needs help both in understanding what is going on and in coping with it, as the following examples point out. The first is a simple situation of opposition to a beginning priest. The second is a more complex situation where the beginning priest had to cope with anger that was directed more at his role than at his person.

Father R was assigned to a parish and, among other duties, was given charge of coordinating pastoral efforts for the elderly and infirm. While the charge was no more definite than that, some parishioners had very concrete expectations. Among them was a man who had definite ideas about the needs of the elderly and who had suggested that hiring a social worker skilled in working with the elderly would be more productive than bringing in a new priest. He repeated this suggestion at each meeting Father R called to look into the needs of the elderly. Father R was taken aback at having to spend part of each meeting justifying his presence in the parish. When the pastor heard of the opposition he went to the next meeting, recognized the value of having a social worker on the staff, said he had considered it, and had decided that a priest like Father R was more valuable to the parish. He asked that they give to him the assistance they would give to the pastor himself. He added that Father R's education was such that they were fortunate to be able to have him on the parish staff, and he, himself, wanted to take this opportunity to welcome him to the parish. With this public support from the pastor, the problem ceased.

The pastor, in this case, brought his authority to bear in support of Father R. In effect he said that Father R was his man and that he wanted the opposition to stop. Had he not done so, Father R's position would have been undermined because the opposition was real. Further, the opposition presupposed that the man who was making the objections had a right to do so, and Father R was implicitly acknowledging this right by granting him the forum to voice the opposition. By this acknowledgment he was ultimately pulling out his own supports from underneath himself, for he was not there at the request of the people or as their employee. He was there because his bishop had assigned him there. Without discussing the appropriateness of the Church's current monarchic system we can nonetheless note that the pastor recognized Father R's need to be defended and protected as a public official of this system. Further, he needed to be defended against his own egalitarian tendencies because they were leading him to serious misreading of his role and position.

In the second example of the need for protection, Father L, newly assigned to a parish, was given the responsibility of liaison with the parish school's parents' association. At one of his first monthly meetings, because of financial pressure, he was given the task of announcing that either tuition was going to be raised or that some school program would have to be cut back. The response was a howl of protest from the parents. Father L pointed out that there was only so much money and that the parish staff was willing to allocate it as the parents' association decided. Father L saw this as a generous and forward move. One parent informed him that if the clergy had been spending their time doing what they were ordained to do instead of worrying about forward moves "then you wouldn't have gotten us and the Church into the mess we're in." Another equally incensed parent said that Father L "should just wait until you need something from us, and then you'll see what it feels like." Most of the other comments were equally angry and personal and nothing was said in Father L's defense. He left the meeting feeling beaten and bewildered. He was especially upset that at the beginning of his ministry so many of his people should be angry at him, for with this sort of beginning the future looked bleak.

In this example, Father L was in need of protection, but protection of a special kind. He needed to be protected from a normal human response, that of personalizing criticism. It was neither possible nor desirable to protect Father L from people's angers and frustrations in their life within the Church. These feelings and attitudes are as much a part of any priest's ministry as any of the people's problems or sufferings. It is quite possible, however, to help a beginning priest see that the sort of anger and frustration that was being expressed during Father L's meeting is not personal. The people were angry and upset with the changes in the Church, and frustrated over their inability to control an important area of their lives, the education of their children. And the anger came out. However, it was not directed to Father L personally but to Father L as a priest.

When a man is on the receiving end of this anger, the distinction between his person and his public role may make for small comfort, but it is important nonetheless. People's relationships to authority and to people in authority are frequently stormy. Learning how to grow beyond the alternating rebellion and submission of the child to an adult position in which cooperation with a public authority can be chosen, not as a personal defeat but as a reasonable choice, is a difficult process. It is equally important, for the individual whose relationship to authority is underdeveloped will be hampered in his relationship with the greatest authority of all, God Himself. For Father L to take people's criticism personally would not only harm him but it would harm them as well. It would keep them on a level of antagonistic relationships with authority in which the only options are resentful submission or rebellion. For Father L to depersonalize the anger, to see it as a very human response to a bad situation, and to help them go beyond it to a choice of possible alternatives would help them to grow in their authority relationships. The protection Father L needed in this case was from the very common human reaction of personalizing conflict. It is a more complex form of protection, but necessary for anyone who is to be in a public position which inevitably attracts criticism.

The beginning priest also needs to feel competent in his work. Feeling at sea and unknowing in the face of varied and complex demands can undermine his sense of competence. He needs assistance in learning how to bring his strengths, his learning, and his idealism to bear on the demands he encounters in his ministry. We have discussed how this assistance can be offered effectively in our section of the models for entry.

Finally, the beginning priest has a need to find his new work gratifying. This is often rendered more difficult by the fact that beginning priests are frequently given less gratifying work. Because the need for gratification is common to all the staff we can expect that the more established staff will be involved in the gratifying work. By chance or by design the new man can end up in less gratifying work, usually less gratifying than he needs. As a result he is deprived of a needed support. This, too, can hinder him in the process of becoming an insider in his pastoral setting.

We can note that the beginning priest has definite areas of need which prove to be of notable importance as he tries to work into his new life. If these needs are not met the result is frustration and a sense of failure which can lead him to question the appropriateness of his vocational choice. He can easily begin to doubt his own abilities, and the chances are that he will begin to question himself before he brings to question the objective difficulty of the situation. It proves to be helpful when he is shown that normal informational needs were not met, that the organizational chart and chain of command don't tell the whole story, that the organizational goals probably don't match the goals of the personnel, and that he can be expected to have certain emotional needs for which fulfillment is quite valid. Pinpointed difficulties prove to be less insurmountable than vaguely difficult situations. Further, articulated needs can be addressed and frequently met. Unarticulated or generic feelings of need often prove too nebulous to be met. The beginning priest needs help both in surfacing his needs and in seeing to their resolution. It is very easy to lose sight of the fact that he is starting out on a life that is public, highly visible, frequently criticized, and often quite lonely. Moving into this work and this life is objectively difficult, and the task of affiliation is accomplished only with effort, and frequently stressful effort.

While the process of affiliation is made much easier when the needs we have just mentioned are surfaced and met, this does not mean that there will be an automatic ease of entry. The capacity of the pastoral setting to absorb outsiders is another real issue. A pastoral setting and the individuals in it are not quite coextensive. There is more to the setting as an operational force than the immediate concerns of those who are visibly at work in it. With all the best will in the world, some situations just won't work. The following examples illustrate the varying capacities of a pastoral setting to absorb newcomers.

Father G began his work in a Catholic Family Assistance program. The program served Spanish-speaking people. The staff of the program worked well together with a minimum of internal friction. At the time Father G joined the staff it was in real need of a representative to other public and private assistance groups as well as to ethnic political groups. Further, the staff was all professionally certified but their certification was very "anglo." They needed a stamp of approval from a source trusted in the Spanish-speaking communities they served. Finally, the program was a training program and was looking for qualified trainees for in-service training.

Father G was fluent in both Spanish and English. He was intelligent and an outgoing, friendly man with an ability to think on his feet. He believed in both the social and religious value of the Family Assistance program. Consequently, he took on the role of the liaison man which he fulfilled well. The Roman collar gave him an authority and a visibility that the lay staff lacked. His own Spanish-speaking background and his priestly role were familiar signposts to the man foreign-born families in the area so he was able to help them utilize the services offered. Finally he, too, wanted to counsel and assist families in need and was able to fit into the program's in-service training.

The program director was able to outline his expectations of Father G, come up with a clear contract, and introduce him to the rest of the staff. For many of the staff this was their first close contact with a priest and a number asked his help in their own personal and religious questions.

Here we see an instance where a pastoral institution was able to absorb an outsider quickly and profitably. The needs they had and the assets he brought meshed well. This is not to say that the situation was without stress. Father G found that becoming an instant representative of the Church also made him an instant target for a lot of personal resentments as well as more broad-based anti-clericalism. But he and the staff were able to understand that they all were involved in a major social process, the change from an English-speaking, largely white community to a Spanish-speaking community of recent immigrants. One of their major roles was to absorb a lot of the stress and frustration that came with this change.

Despite the built-in stress and the dimensions of the social problems the organization was able to absorb the newcomer with little difficulty. The ease came more from the nature of the situation than from the personnel. The director needed someone. He had been looking for a Spanish-speaking priest, preferably one from the same background as the people in the area, and Father G fit the bill. There was work for him to do that no one else was doing. Not only was he not taking away someone else's work, but, by his public relations work, he was helping to guarantee their job security.

By contrast, there is the situation of Father A. He, too, was working in a Catholic institution. Although he worked well and learned from his work he remained essentially an outsider never managing to crack through the shell of resistance presented by the insiders. Again, the reasons were largely structural and independent of the personal relationships Father A maintained with the staff, which were cordial and even friendly.

The institution had been founded after the First World War to meet the social needs of Catholic immigrant families. At one point, the institution was in a state of transition because of the changes in immigration laws. A new director had been appointed a year before

Father A's arrival to deal with the question of the institution's future.

Many staff members had been there a long time. They were used to the old ways and services and were in favor of seeking out a new clientele who could use their services. The director, with the encouragement of his board of trustees, was in favor of shifting the institution's focus to new groups with new needs. Traditionally, the director had always been a priest, and successful directors often advanced upwards in the ranks of the clergy. Because the anticipated changes might mean job changes, the staff were busy building their case loads as a way of showing that the old services were still needed.

Everyone, employees and director, expressed a desire to have Father A on the staff. But each, it turned out, wanted him for something different. The director wanted an ally in his job in bringing about change. The staff wanted help in rounding up clientele for the old services. But they also wanted the clients, who were in short supply, for themselves. Further, with the possibility that fewer clients might mean fewer jobs the older staff did not want any new competition.

Father A was given an office, a telephone, a supervisor, and was asked to all staff meetings and given all the privileges of staff membership. The only thing he was not given was any work. He was free to go out and round up any clients he could, provided he did not trespass on the territory of one of the staff. But since the area had been all divided up among the staff, anywhere he went was on someone's territory. At one point, he noted that the one place on no one's list was the lobby of the city jail. The supervisor, with apparent seriousness, replied that "maybe he should think about the lobby."

Father A was an outsider and he stayed an outsider. The institution was not in any position to help him, or anyone else for that matter, become an insider. The insiders, the staff, were doing their utmost to keep another outsider, the director, from getting inside with his new ideas and plans. Despite Father A's graciousness and consistently friendly relationships with all, he remained an outsider. At one point, when he commented that "there's no work around here," he was quickly given several on-going clients just enough to silence his criticism and keep him somewhat busy, but not enough to incorporate him into the staff.

A third example further illustrates some of the problems a staff can encounter in trying to bring a newcomer into the inner circle of staff membership. Father C was a pleasant, somewhat shy young man who was hard working and who functioned well in a structured setting. His work setting was an inner city parish with a large staff of experienced and able priests and sisters. They expressed an initial desire to have him join their staff and the prospect for his work there seemed promising.

From the very beginning, Father C began to receive negative reactions from the staff, most of which was centered on their inability to provide the structures he needed. However, the speed with which these negative reactions surfaced and the strength of the responses were all out of proportion to his visibility and significance on the staff.

An examination of the staff's structure revealed several facts. There was only one full-time priest and one full-time brother on the staff. There were two part-time priests who had staff responsibilities but whose full-time work in the diocese was significant and demanding of both time and energy. There were several part-time volunteer seminarians, and a part-time sister who also volunteered her services. Each of these volunteers also had major responsibilities in the parish and functioned well. The part-time volunteers outnumbered the pastor six to one and they outnumbered the regular staff two to one. The pastor and his assistant were doing an admirable job of supervising this string of part-time helpers and managing all the parish resources. Despite a chronic and severe shortage of funds, a situation of social change, a high incidence of family instability, and all the other ills that affect the inner city, the staff was able to present good liturgies that met the needs of the people, run an inventive and competent grade school, and address itself to the many-faceted needs of its people both spiritually and economically. In large part this was due to the pastor's efforts at holding all the strings of volunteer part-time help together. Each volunteer received time and direction. He stayed calm and kept everyone's fingers off panic buttons by dealing with crisis in a rational, low-keyed, and orderly way.

But the man was achieving these goals by working to full capacity, both physically and emotionally. Father C's arrival threatened to become the straw that might break this particular camel's back. The staff had already absorbed more outsiders than most staffs would be able to absorb. They were producing on a higher level than would normally be expected. They had neither the energy reserve nor the time to assist still another beginner to become part of their staff.

The process of affiliation or of becoming an insider, in summary, is not only a crucial task but a difficult one. It requires that the difficulty be recognized, and that the new man be given the support necessary to cope with the difficulty. This entails meeting certain very real needs. It also involves an analysis of whether or not the particular pastoral setting is able to absorb a newcomer. And it means that the process of entry be seen as a process, and not just a single event whose completion is assured by the fact of ordination.

Learning To Think Contractually

At the beginning of this chapter we mentioned three major tasks facing the priest as he begins his pastoral work. The first was the task of affiliation. The second is the task of learning to think contractually. This proves to be a major challenge, both in his work setting and in his work with people.

The existence of a workable contract is quite possibly the single most important element facing the beginning priest. It is also, in all probability, the most overlooked. While this may sound like an extravagant claim the following examples will illustrate the importance both of the contract itself and of the ability to understand it, or the ability to think contractually. While the word contract usually refers to a written agreement, we use it here to connote an unwritten and implicit agreement.

Father R, a member of a religious order, was assigned to a parish maintained by the order. His assignment came from the regional superior. He was an accomplished musician and had long looked forward to ordination and the opportunity to utilize his talents in presenting creative liturgies. The regional superior was of a similar mind and thought that these abilities would complement the solid but rather unimaginative approach of the current parish staff. Father R arrived with high hopes. The pastor welcomed him, noted that there was much work to be done in the parish, was pleased to have a young man with drive and energy on the staff, and gave him his list of assignments which were standard parish responsibilities.

Little by little, Father R's hopes turned to apprehensions. Nothing was changing, the liturgies were remaining the same, his advice was gently rejected, and he found no outlet for his talents. Feeling as though the anticipated changes were being unilaterally postponed by the pastor, his frustration increased and he finally exploded in an angry attack on the pastor.

An analysis of the situation revealed that the pastor had never been consulted in any of the anticipated changes and did not want them. He had asked for help and had been given a newly ordained priest. He had assumed, as had been the case in his own first assignment, that he, as pastor, would tell the young man what to do and that the new man would do as he was told. Further, he noted that he was a canonical pastor and superior and that Church law, tradition, and the practice of the diocese supported him in his view of his rights. Father R, on the other hand, had read the interest and encouragement of the regional superior as a green light for work in the liturgy. He assumed that this had all been arranged with the pastor. The superior, for his part, assumed that the pastor would be just as anxious to put Father R's talents to work as he, the superior, was anxious to see them put to work. He further assumed that Father R and the pastor "would work things out." In this instance, each man had a definite set of expectations, but in each case it was assumed that they were not different, that they were both common and clearly understood.

As we can see in this situation, which is reenacted in the Church time and time again, expectations and assumptions are real, functional, and unstated. We all have expectations, and assume that others can read our minds. It is common to hear people say "well it ought to be obvious that. . . ." It is safer to assume nothing until it is made clear, and to recognize that nothing is obvious until it is made so explicitly.

In addition to personal expectations it is common for expectations to be worked into the fabric of an institution. Most parishes and pastoral institutions have developed ways of doing things, and the new man often doesn't find out what these are until a violation leads him to be told that "That's not the way we do things here."

In Father W's first assignment he was asked to hear daily confessions at 7:30 in the morning. After dressing he would sit in the dining room reading the morning paper over a cup of coffee until shortly before 7:30 and then go over to the church, arriving right at 7:30. He noted that something must be wrong for the pastor was showing signs of increasing irritation. Finally, the pastor told Father W that he should stop being so lazy and get to the church when the people got there. Perplexed, Father W said that he was never late and gave people as much time as they needed. The pastor, still angry, added that his people were mostly poor and hardworking, that they could lose their jobs if they were late to work, and that for twenty years the priests in the parish had prided themselves on having confessions over by 7:30, not starting at 7:30. Father W was more than willing to go along with this and do what was expected of him. He only wanted someone to spell out what he was to do. However, the pastor's protest that "we've always done it that way in this parish and everyone in town knows it" was not particularly helpful since Father W's assignment to the parish also marked his initial visit to the town.

Father J was asked on occasion to take one of the older priest's day on duty when the older man wished to go somewhere on his assigned work day. He agreed willingly, stating that helping each other out was a nice way to work. On one occasion when he wished to go away he asked the older man to cover for him and was taken aback by the sputtering indignation that ensued. Again, it was the unwritten rule that the older men had the right to ask the newest assistant to do their work for them on occasion, but that he did not have the right to ask them to do his.

In entering into his first assignment the new priest should go in with the question in his mind, "What is the contract here?" Assuredly, there are certain things he is supposed to do and certain things he is not supposed to do. There are people he is to visit and certain people he is not supposed to visit. There is in all probability "a way we do things around here." Further, we may anticipate that most clergy find it difficult to recognize this reality and spell out its details. It is not easy for a pastor to tell his new assistant that he is not equal and that he, as pastor, has rights to gratification and reward that the junior man does not have. Because of the religious value placed on service and equality, articulating privileges and special rights does not come easy to the clergy.

For whatever reason the clergy often find it difficult to recognize that the real situation falls short of stated ideals. As a result, the stated goals can conflict with the actual ones embodied in the unwritten contract. The following incident typically illustrates this. Father N joined the staff of a campus ministry. In his first meeting with the staff they explained that they had a team ministry and wanted him to be sure to work as a part of the team. He had several interests including retreat programs and liturgies. As he spoke of his desire to implement these interests he was informed that the weekend retreats were an area in which Father L was in charge, that Father W and a group of students planned the liturgies, and that if he really wished to get things accomplished it would be better to meet privately with the responsible people. Putting this information together Father N came up with a picture of a pastoral effort that was divided into a distinct number of relatively noncommunicating categories with a different staff member in charge. In effect, he was expected to carve out his own piece of the turf, not tread on anyone else's turf, and in return would receive exclusive right to his own territory. Once he was able to recognize that this really was the unwritten contract and the one in effect, that the talk about team ministry was just that, talk, and that the turf system was a standard and workable, if not ideal, pastoral method, Father N was able to go to work in an effective manner.

We can note the importance of unwritten contracts in pastoral work. In addition to any possible written contract there is an unwritten contract which covers most of the significant areas. Further, all the individuals had their own unstated expectations which are as important as the collective expectations. Understanding the unwritten contract increases the new priest's ability to cope with his new work. Observing the unwritten contract will help make the working and living situation manageable. Violating it or changing it unilaterally—and a unilateral change is a violation—will make for problems in both the working and living situation.

In addition to recognizing the contract on the institutional level, the beginning priest needs to think contractually in his work with people. What this means quite simply is that the help that people are seeking from him and the help he offers must come together. A common source of failure in pastoral work is that the help sought and the help offered do not come together, i.e., there is not a contract as in the following situation.

A middle-aged couple asked to see Father D. After specialized training in marriage counseling he was newly assigned to a parish. The woman was very upset because her seventeen-year-old daughter had left home and was living with a young man in a hippy commune. The father, equally upset, was also distraught at his wife's frequent angry outbursts at the other children and at him. Father D, noting the tension between the couple, suggested that some work on their relationship might be helpful. The husband agreed willingly and the sessions began. The woman continued to focus almost exclusively and angrily on her daughter's desertion and after two sessions never came again. The subsequent sessions with the husband ended inconclusively and disappointingly, and the counseling was discontinued.

In looking into the situation it became clear that the woman, quite simply, wanted Father D to go to the daughter, upbraid her for her wicked ways, and bring her home. The husband wanted peace and quiet in his house and wanted him to bring this about. He was trying to do marriage counseling. The three individuals, the man and woman and Father D, were going in different directions which never met. Father D was anxious to use his new skills, skills in which the woman had no interest. The couple wanted him to be the authoritarian priest, but each wanted him to use that authority in a different way. Father D was trying to be the counselor. Needless to say, the situation was doomed from the beginning.

In another situation, Father P was asked to visit a number of sick and elderly parishioners as part of a parish program in home visiting. The pastor had been visiting them, and Father P believed in the value of the program and also wished to please the pastor. He went to each person on the list, chatted for awhile, and then asked whether he could do anything for them. About half said no, one elderly man told him that he was out of milk and would appreciate it if Father P would get him some. A few needed rides to the doctor, and one woman, after talking about the death of her husband, launched into an attack on the changes in the Church. Father P was as baffled by the variety of the responses as he was puzzled over what to do about them. With help he came to understand that there were several contracts involved. First, there was his contract with the pastor, namely, that he would visit the people on the list. Unfortunately, there had been no discussion with the pastor about what he should do once he got inside the front door. Since it was apparently obvious, he was too embarrassed to ask the pastor. He knew that it was important because the pastor had said that "home visiting helps build community." so he knew that whatever home visiting might be, it was certainly important. This did not cast much light on what he should do once the front door was opened but it certainly raised his level of anxiety about it.

81

With help, Father P came to see that the contract with the pastor and the contract with the parishioners were different. Further, there would be a different contract with each of the parishioners he might visit. The help he would have to offer might be the same, but the help sought would quite understandably differ from person to person. Consequently, there would be a need to arrange a working contract, i.e., bring together with each person the help sought and the help offered.

In this, as in almost all pastoral situations, there is a structured introduction to the relationship. The notion of home visiting was in this case that structured introduction. But once the introduction has served its purpose there is a need to work out a contract. Learning to think contractually, learning to understand that there is a need to articulate what help is being offered and what help is being sought, to estimate whether the two can be brought together, and if they cannot, what alternatives there are, is a major learning issue for the beginning priest.

Pastoral situations can be understood and they require analysis. To assume that things are clear before an attempt is made to clarify them is unrealistic. Most pastoral situations, even the traditional roles, require a serious effort at clarification. Learning to think contractually involves learning to ask clarifying questions. Why is this person seeking me out? Why did he come here at this particular point in time? What is his concept of help? What is his previous experience with help? What role does he associate with a priest? What help does he think I have to offer? What help do I, in fact, have to offer him and can I offer him what he is looking for? Does he really want my help or has he come here only to please someone else?

Because many priestly relationships are ritualized, it is possible to get into a pastoral situation and have a ritualized relationship carry both priest and parishioner through the motions of doing something. Oftentimes these relationships can end inconclusively without either person recognizing that they didn't really know why they were working together. There is a certain value in going through motions when these motions are sacred and have a symbolic value in themselves. However, when the question at hand is not a rite but an attempt to achieve something, then going through motions is not particularly helpful, as the following example illustrates.

Father R was assigned direction of his new parish's teenage club. The pastor told him that working with teenagers was important, and that it was a means to help young people stay in the Church. Father R showed up at the first weekly meeting and found a large number of young people there. The pastor had made an announcement that the new priest would be meeting with the teenagers and had urged parents to send their children. At the first meeting a vocal girl said that they had a president last year but that the president graduated from high school and was now going to college in a distant city. Father R then suggested that they elect officers and the election process, which took several weekly meetings, began. At the third weekly meeting the number of young people had fallen to one-half the original number. Distressed by this, he asked those in attendance what had happened. A discussion began and it soon became clear that most of the young people didn't really know why they were there other than that their parents wanted them to be there. One of them asked him why he was there and he, laughingly, blurted out "because the pastor told me to be here." They realized at this point that they were all going through the motions of a meeting to please someone else. The priest was there because the pastor told him to be there. The children were there because their parents told them to be there. And they had begun to elect officers without realizing that they had nothing for the officers to do because they had no goals. The group existed by mandate, but there was no real purpose behind the mandate.

Collectively they were being carried along by the structure of a weekly meeting. There was a place for them to meet, a time to begin and a time to end, and an expectation that they be there and that they do something. In this particular case they were able to recognize this and actually establish a working contract. It would not have been atypical for the weekly meetings to continue without a contract, but instead carried by the structure.

Establishing Pastoral Identity

The third of the three tasks we mentioned at the beginning of this chapter is the need to establish a pastoral identity. This can also be seen as the discovery of the style of pastoral ministry that works for each man. In part this is dictated by personality or temperament. But in large measure it results from trying out different roles. Fortunately, the need to exercise these different roles arises fairly soon in the course of most pastoral work. Unfortunately, the fact that the roles differ, and the way they differ are not always recognized. When they are, an understanding is brought about of the relationships that are part of the role and the expectations that go with it. We can illustrate these roles with the following examples.

Father M had two requests presented to him shortly after he arrived in his first assignment, and reported having very strong feelings about each. In the first, during a Saturday afternoon confession, a parishioner presented him with a dilemma and asked him what to do. Father M suggested that they look at the alternatives. The man said this wasn't necessary: "Just tell me what is right, what to do, and I'll do it." In a state of increasing discomfort, he tried to help the man make his own decision, but to no avail. The individual wanted a clear-cut directive from the priest. Finally at the end, and feeling very uncomfortable, he suggested an alternative rather halfheartedly and the confession ended inconclusively and painfully for each.

In another situation Father M was asked by an old, former parishioner who had moved to a distant town to look up the man's childhood friend. He had heard that the man, still living in the parish, was ill and in need. He knew the man's first name only and the name of a cousin. There was no more definite information than that. He went to see the town clerk; together they went over the town records and, by sleuthing and good guesswork, located the man. Father M went to visit him and discovered a tough, eccentric, and very independent old man living in a shrub-hidden cabin. He was in bad health and suffering from an inadequate diet. With great sensitivity to the man's lifelong independence and his insistence that "none of them damn do-gooders come poking around in my house," Father M managed to get him medical care and a better diet and to bring some order to the cabin. Eventually, there was even a religious request from the old man. Father M reported that he enjoyed the old man's company, looked on the situation as a challenge, and experienced a great sense of accomplishment in what he was able to do.

In these two incidents we can see two different but traditional roles that are placed on the newly ordained. In the first, Father M was asked to be the lawgiver. He was asked to give a command by an individual who was prepared to obey. In the second he was asked to find and bring help to an old man with a physical need. He was asked to function in the role of a social worker.

What is significant here is the difference in his emotional reaction to the two roles. He was very comfortable in the role of social worker. He was extremely uncomfortable in the role of lawgiver. The difference in these reactions should come as no great surprise, for the quality of the relation structured into each role is quite different. Any priest, either by reason of temperament or personal situation, is going to find some types of relationships difficult. The expectations, responsibilities, and demands of some roles and the relationships built into them, are going to feel uncomfortable. To understand this more concretely we will look at several priestly roles and the type of relationship that is associated with each.

Without pretending that this list is exhaustive or precise we will list six different priestly roles. In addition to the two mentioned above, the lawgiver and social worker roles, we can distinguish the teaching role, the prophetic role, the counselor's role, and the role of the ritualist or priest in the narrowest sense.

Each of these roles uses its own medium for relating and seeks to achieve its own, distinct goal. The lawgiver role uses command as the medium of relationship and seeks to establish a state of obedience. To the objection that you must obey something and not just obey abstractly, we can add that the relationship of obedience to an authority figure, regardless of the issue, is a reality for some people. The social worker relates by means of the assistance he brings an individual and his goal is to establish the individual's well-being. The teacher relates by means of his special knowledge. By giving this knowledge to others he seeks to give them the means to act purposefully. He acts in the belief that knowledge increases moral responsibility. The prophetic role brings moral judgments to bear on society, singling out moral failing, injustice, or hypocrisy. Here the goal is conversion, a change of heart and a change of actions, from wrong-doing to what is right. The counselor uses the very relationship itself as a means of bringing about a change in the way of relating to the individual or group one is working with. Usually this is in the area of troubled or troubling feelings in some area of life that has proven not only injurious but usually alienating. Not only does the counselor seek to change the feeling tone of the individual but also to overcome the sense of alienation.

Finally, there is the priestly role in the narrow sense, or the role of the ritualist. Probably the most visible of the pastor's roles, it is also the most complex. We will discuss this in greater detail than the other roles because it proves to be the role that is most troubling to the beginning priest. The feelings stirred up within its scope, and the situations associated with it, provide some of the more unsettling experiences faced by the beginning priest. Further, the way these feelings and situations are resolved will often affect the way in which his pastoral identity is firmed up.

In this particular role the priest relates by means of rite or rituals. Because ritual, with its primitive and almost magical aspects, appeals in an almost universal way to a fundamental part of the human psyche, we run the risk of major distortion in assigning any simple goal to its functioning. Nonetheless, we will attempt an explanation. Italian author Luigi Barzini has said that "the savage beast in the heart of Man" is tamed not by reason but by ritual. This description is as apt as it is poetic. It goes to the heart of the matter for it speaks of man's need to order the primitive and disorderly part of himself. Our rituals bring order, acceptability, and healing. Instincts like aggressiveness and sexuality, events like illness, birth and death, and many feelings like guilt and sorrow, are often too powerful to be dealt with alone and too real to be denied. The priest, by using his rituals, restores order in the life of the individual who has been overwhelmed by emotion or instinct. He brings social healing and integration to feelings or situations which, because of their power, threaten isolation.

As the examples used at the beginning of the section indicate, people have different reactions to the different roles. The differences stem from the quality of the relationships common to each role. The lawgiver relates in a parental way. The counselor relates in a personal way. The teacher relates with clarity of thought, though his personality may remain private. While different individuals will adapt to these roles and their different ways of relating with varying degrees of ease and difficulty, there is a rather common difficulty in relating to the more primitive aspects of the ritualist's role. To begin with, it seems magical, and magic is highly suspect. Religious ceremonies with little rational content, which seem impersonal or where there is little sense of fellowship, cause considerable discomfort to many a newly ordained priest. Those rites which approach to the more primitive aspects of the sacred and holy are often sources of stress.

An obvious reason for this is that, with the exception of his own ordination, he has not been exposed to those life situations which utilize rituals. Many young priests have not yet experienced the death of a parent or close relative during which time the value of funeral rites can become evident. Obviously, he has not had the experience of seeing his own children baptized. He has not experienced the sacralizing effect of a wedding ceremony.

Rituals can be effective in coping with fairly primitive instincts. And, as we noted above, it is ritual that tames the savage beast in man, not reason. But little of the savage beast has shown up in the life of a newly ordained priest. He has had to cope with his own aggressive and sexual instincts, but these are effectively handled through suppression or some form of constructive outward channeling. The deep feelings stirred up by death, crushing defeat, or rejection, and the sense of impotence and inadequacy that comes with these experiences are often still far from his world. Consequently, the sacred rituals which help people troubled by these experiences have less meaning for him.

Almost invariably, the first year of pastoral work will bring the newly ordained priest in contact with situations in which the use of rituals is not only appropriate but often the only thing that really works. At these times, instances in which he is ministering to bereaved or overwhelmed people, he will discover the power and symbolic value that attaches both to the rituals and to his role as a priest. Surprisingly enough, and almost invariably, this discovery is unsettling. It is unsettling because it involves a new and different way of relating. Significantly this new way involves greater distance, and it brings unanticipated feelings of responsibility. It is new, it is powerful, and it often comes as a great surprise. Frequently, this discovery is the source of considerable stress.

An example can be found in the following incident. A young woman, described by her doctor as marginally psychotic, and who was still under psychiatric care, came to Father O with the request that he write a letter to her boyfriend. The young man was in the Army in the Pacific and had recently written suggesting that they should postpone their projected marriage. The girl was panicked by the suggestion, and told Father O that the marriage had to take place. She asked him to write her fiancee and tell him that they should get married. She told him that this would work because "you're a priest." Above and beyond the young woman's rather tenuous grasp on reality, which he found difficult to cope with, Father O was bothered by the expectation that "because I'm a priest I can do anything." With the help of his supervisor, he came to see that he was being asked to assume the role of magician, a role which has often been associated with the priesthood. He was reluctant to assume this role, and was able to see that there were a number of parishioners, obviously more stable than the young girl, who also seemed to think he could perform magical rites. His prayers were expected to heal marital disharmony, get children off narcotics, heal illness, and secure employment. It was helpful to Father O to have a label put on this particular role expectation. Further, it was helpful for him to see that his was indeed one of the traditional (culturally, not theologically traditional) priestly roles, but that it was not required that he feel comfortable in it nor assume it. To know that there is such a thing as magical thinking, that the Church over the years has maintained an uneasy truce with people's magical thinking, but that the single priest was not required to be the Church's agent of that truce was both a surprise and a relief.

It is, as noted above, unrealistic to expect that a priest will be able to assume all these roles effectively and with equal ease. The differences between them are too great. We noted above the ease with which Father M assumed the role of social worker and his distress in the role of lawgiver. The lawgiver's role is a very paternal and authoritative one, a role sufficiently different from that of the seminarian. Many a young priest needs considerable time and experience to help him grow into it. The social worker's role, on the contrary, is one to which many seminarians are exposed in the course of their studies, as was Father M who had spent several months working for a state welfare program as a deacon.

Each of these roles, with the differing degrees of closeness and distance it requires, its different medium of relationship and consequently an overall difference in the quality of the relationship it builds upon, is quite different from the other roles. Unfortunately, the differences are almost never recognized. Father T, shortly after being assigned to an inner-city parish, reported receiving requests from three separate individuals who sought him out "as a priest." The first, a middle-aged woman with a Catholic college background, was troubled by recent changes in the Church and needed, in effect, several private tutorial sessions in current theology (as well as the obvious need to ventilate her anger at changing things without asking her). Given the theological rationales for the changes she went away satisfied, if not happy. The second, a woman whose "children were going bad" and whose life in many ways was starting to fall apart, came looking for prayers and support. Father T prayed with and for her, and supported her efforts to get on top of her situation. The third, a lonely and depressed young man, came looking for an alternative to loneliness. Father T established a counseling relationship with him and helped him join several parish groups.

In each of these three situations, the individual wanted the help of a priest. But the definition of help was role-defined, and the role was different in each case. The first wanted a teacher. The second wanted a ritualist who would validate and bring God's support to her efforts to hold on. The third needed a counselor. Each of these roles is different from the others and requires a different way of relating. In the first situation Father T related not as a superior but more as a peer giving answers to questions and treating all questions as valid. In the second he had to draw on the sacral strengths of the priestly role itself and relate through the medium of that role. He was much more authoritative and definite as a way of structuring support. In the third situation he was more personally involved and was conscious of the human side of his relationship with the young man. These three pastoral situations required that he shift gears considerably. Being helped to recognize the different roles and what was expected in each proved a notable assistance to him in assuming these roles.

These different priestly roles are all appropriate for priests and are common in the Church. A major task of the beginning priest is working out an understanding of the roles he can assume and the ones he cannot assume. Further, he needs the assistance of the senior clergy in coming to this understanding. Not only does he need help in recognizing the roles for what they are, he needs permission not to take on the ones he can't handle. Otherwise, the experience can prove a major personal defeat instead of the constructive recognition of limitations that it could and should be. Used constructively, role identifying can be a major assistance in helping him give concrete shape to his own priestly identity.

Pastoral role problems involve more than determining which role feels comfortable. It is not unusual for the beginning priest to feel uncomfortable in assuming any role. Prior to ordination the priest was a private individual, and he may wish to preserve that accustomed situation. In shrinking from assuming any role the newly ordained priest is instinctively recognizing that the assumption of a role involves change in a sensitive area. Quite rightly he knows that assuming a public and religious role can change the relationships he already has and that it will require a new way of relating.

An example of change in the quality of relationship is related by Father L. Shortly after he started his work in his new parish assignment he was approached by an old friend. This friend and Father L had known each other since they were school children together. Their friendship in recent years had been a source of real support for Father L, although the demands of seminary life had meant that their contacts were less frequent. Now that he was ordained he anticipated more mobility and with that mobility the opportunity to see more of his old friends.

When this man telephoned requesting an appointment to talk about something personal, Father L was taken aback. He knew instinctively that this would entail a change in their relationship. Heretofore, their relationship was a private one which did not take Father L's new role into account. He wished to keep it that way. He said that he, too, needed support in his work and looked for this support from his friends. He was afraid lest whatever come up in the interview change the quality of the relationship from that of friendship to a professional one.

Father L's fears were on target. The request for help changed the quality of an old relationship. It also established a new sort of relationship, one that felt strange to the beginning priest. It is difficult for an individual who has spent all his life being a private person to realize that he has taken on a role which many view as more significant than he is. Further, many people have strong feelings about their role. To be a public representative of the Roman Catholic Church, which claims to speak with the authority of God Himself, and which frequently does speak on issues which touch people's lives, is to be in a very difficult position. Almost by definition there will be criticism and attack. But most important, it is definitely to be in a role that goes far beyond the dimensions of the person himself.

Beginning priests report that the public identification of them as representatives of the Church is overwhelming. Unfortunately, they often believe that there is a way to function which will not bring about rejection, criticism, or any of the negative feedback which proves so difficult to absorb. This is just plain wrong. There is no way for a pastorally active priest to avoid criticism and all the discomfort that goes with a controversial role.

To begin with, it is difficult to move from being a private individual to being a public one. Under the best of circumstances it is difficult because the reactions and responses which worked for the private individual are now inadequate. In order to survive in that role an individual must learn a new set of reactions. Learning these reactions and going through the experiences in which they are learned is indeed a difficult process. There is no way in which it can be made easy. The loss of that refuge, which goes with being a private individual, and the acceptance of an identification, which follows the individual wherever he goes, is painful and burdensome. The only way this burden can be lightened is through the recognition that while the role is difficult there is a distinction between the role and the person.

Further, it is impossible to assume a role which is identified with a normative and ancient institution without having to deal with people's feelings about that institution. For better or worse, the new priest is a representative of the Church, and he must cope with the fact that many people dislike the Church and everything about it.

Not all reactions to the role is negative. Many beginning priests report that they are granted recognition and privileges as priests which had not been given to them before their ordination. Often, they find this as difficult to cope with as the negative responses.

This is frequently articulated as the desire not to become a professional cleric, or "that sort of priest." In reality, what they are experiencing is the same discomfort in this new role.

Principles for Work Selection

Another part of his view of himself as a pastor is the choice of principles for selecting his work. Deciding which work he will do and which he will not do, what work is his responsibility and which is not, when he should accept a request and when he may or even should say no are important decisions. Frequently the new priest hasn't even thought about these questions, but the press of demands forces him into it. Often it is the time and energy spent in some bizarre task that makes him think about what work he should and should not be doing. There are some built in answers to these questions, answers that have been at work in the life of the American Church for many years. We can list the principles of selection and then see how they work in the concrete. The late Chaplain Thomas Klink, who directed the Division of Religion and Psychiatry at the Menninger Foundation in Topeka suggested three principles, and we will follow his division. These are the labor principle, the specialization principle, and the professionalization principle.

When asked what he does, a priest operating according to the labor principle would answer, "Whatever I can." The labor principle was common in rural America and described the situation of the average country pastor. He worked for his people in an indiscriminate manner. Not only did he perform the regular sacramental ministry but he also may have helped to dig graves, provide food and clothing for the poor, teach the children, assist in barn raising or crop gathering, provide transportation, and assist in all those other areas where people needed help. (This model is not wholly of the past. The author of this volume took part in almost all of these activities in a parish in rural Alaska.) Because this has been a traditional American principle for the selection of pastoral work, we can assume that it will appear on occasion in the expectations placed on beginning priests either by the laity or by other priests. The labor principle describes the situation today of many priests working with the urban poor, as the following incident illustrates.

Father D was asked by a parishioner for assistance in finding housing and, once having found it, for the use of the parish truck. He was even asked to be at the wheel in the actual move. The new priest was taken aback by the request and was at a loss whether to say yes or no. He reported the situation as a cause of considerable anxiety, not "because of the work but because of what it means. If I accept every request that comes along, I'll end up a handyman, not a priest." Quite rightly he saw the question as crucial for it required him to come up with a means for choosing the work he would do, i.e., a work selection model. He wanted to help but he wanted to be the one to decide how he was going to help. He needed a rationale to help him decide. His supervisor was able to help him grasp the situation and see that the parishioner saw him functioning under the labor principle. Examining the labor model, Father D decided that he did not want to follow it because it placed too low a value on the years of specialized training he had received and in which he had invested so much of himself. He was then able to come up with an alternative. Calling on emergency funds budgeted by the local, public housing office he made arrangements to have the woman moved by professional movers.

Again, the symbolic dimension of the situation was more important than the situation itself. It involved the choice of a means for discriminating between the work he would do and the work he would refuse. Ordained recently, and idealistic, he wanted to be at the service of his people but wanted to know "whether I've got to do whatever they ask me to do." It came as a relief to learn that, first, he had not only the right but the obligation to set priorities and decide which work to do. Second, meeting a request for help did not require that he accept the request as a description of the way the assistance was to be offered. Third, he should explore the alternatives for help in the case. Father D was also able to recognize, incidentally, the importance and helpfulness of this rationale in helping him cope with this troubling situation.

The second principle for the selection of work is the principle of specialization. Here the pastor chooses his work in accord with his specialized skill or knowledge. This is the situation of the so-called "hyphenated priest," the priest-counselor, or the priest-teacher, or the priest-musician. This man sees himself as a technician. He has a specialization to offer, and does that work which utilizes it. This can be in the area of specialized knowledge, as with priests who teach, or it can be in the area of specialized skills, as with counselors and social scientists. But whatever the area, there is a structure in the method of the specialist which preselects for him the work he will do and the work he will not do.

For the individual who finds the indiscrimination of the labor principle burdensome, the structured limits of a specialization can be most appealing. In addition, they provide the new priest with a pastoral identity that is usually both intelligible and respected. When asked what he does he can respond that he is a professor of theology, or a counselor, or a sociologist. These answers communicate a work that is clearly focused on specific tasks and which is the mark of an educated man. As such, it can be expected to command respect.

The problem with the specialization principle is that it ill suits the pastor. The specialist relates by means of his specialized skill or knowledge. Who and what he is as a person is of only peripheral importance, if even that. Without in any way underestimating the value of the content of his specialization we can still maintain that following the principle of specialization as a way of choosing pastoral work, as the specialist does, is inappropriate for the pastor because it is too narrow and too task-oriented. The specialist is a technician in whose life the function of witness is minimal. In the life of the pastor, witness is of major importance.

The third principle for the selection of pastoral work is the professional principle. As used here the word "professional" does not bespeak something distant or uninvolved or bereft of the spontaneity or the uniqueness of individual human beings. Rather, it refers to the pastor's method of selecting his work, a selection based on an understanding of pastoral goals and the right means to reach these goals. But first, priorities must be set, as the following incident illustrates. Father L was stopped by a parishioner after Sunday Mass and asked whether she and her husband could come to see him about a difficulty they were having. He looked in his appointment book and asked when they would like to come. The woman suggested the following Tuesday night. Father L noted that he had to meet with the parish liturgy committee that night and met with them regularly except in emergencies. Wednesday was his day off and he had already arranged to be away with a friend of his. What about Thursday? The woman responded that she thought it would be good to discuss the matter before Thursday. Father L, noting that they were unable to come in during the daytime, offered to make arrangements for them to meet on the next Tuesday with another member of the staff in whom he had great confidence. The woman was pleased, thanked him for his assistance, and kept the appointment, which proved fruitful.

In this simple incident Father L received a request, quickly established the fact that he had priorities in his work which appeared to take precedence, and offered an alternative which worked. A request was made, an evaluation of alternatives was made, and one of them was selected. He was able to see that meeting the woman's request did not require that he meet it exactly as she had anticipated. As a professional he came in with a different perspective, one which he had the right and even the obligation to introduce. Were he unable to do this, the value in seeking his assistance in the first place would be open to question. The fact that his assistance was sought gave him a right to structure the response. This rather classical case-work principle, known as "professional difference," is as useful and appropriate for the pastor as it is for the social worker, for it gives each one the conceptual tools for analyzing a situation and designing a response based on what will work.

The beginning priest has to come up with a picture of the priesthood that he can fit into and live with. He must establish his own pastoral identity. The broad range of possibilities for traditional and effective priestly work is too broad for any single individual. The recognition that no priest can meet all requests, and more concretely, each beginning priest's recognition that he cannot meet every request made of him, can be the occasion of either a useful role clarification or a personal and professional defeat. It should be a helpful and clarifying experience. In order that it be positive, the beginning priest needs the assistance of responsible and functioning pastors to help him interiorize the principle, which says that help, of its very nature, is limited.

CHAPTER FIVE

crises
of entry

Stress and Anxiety in Pastoral Work

One of the outstanding characteristics of the initial period of pastoral work is that it is a time of anxiety and stress. Quite literally, the beginner is anxious to do well and to make a success of his new work. But success does not come easily. He is faced with a number of stressful situations. He relates to people in new and untried ways. He is given a visibility to which he is unaccustomed. He confronts difficult situations, certain ones for the first time in his life. These elements add up to anxiety and stress. This does not mean that the beginning period need be unpleasant or unrewarding. The contrary is both possible and common. Rather, it means that because of both the objective difficulty of the work and its symbolic value to a large, believing community, stress and anxiety are ordinary working conditions.

It would be useful to determine the causes of anxiety and stress in pastoral work. But this goes beyond our scope. We will identify the stress and anxiety as they occur and try to point out any patterns that show up. In doing so we are involved more in art than in science, and we present our observations in that light. What the observations show is that stress and anxiety surface around several issues that face the beginning priest, and surface with sufficient predictability that we can consider them to be critical issues. These issues end up playing such an important role in the new priest's life that we can call them crisis issues. These issues are the identity-intimacy issue, power and powerlessness, and disillusionment. We will look into each of these after first looking more into the conditions in which these crises surface, the stress and anxiety in the life of the beginning priest, and the way they affect his work and his learning.

How does anxiety affect learning? This is a major question for the beginning priest because stress and anxiety are hallmarks of the initial period of pastoral work. Another characteristic is that this beginning period is a time of learning. The new priest is learning much that is completely new. But the content of his learning is not the only significant element. Equally important is the pattern of interaction with his people in which his knowledge is put to the test.

In the course of his introduction to pastoral work he will learn, quite concretely, what it means for him, as an individual, to be that professional person who, heretofore, has been an abstract ideal for him. Testing himself against that ideal, knowing and fearing that he will make mistakes and that he might fail, is difficult. It makes this period of entry a time of real stress. Because this time is also one of learning in which the stakes are high, the effect of stress on practical learning is an important issue.

Many educators have theories about the effect of stress on the professional's learning during this period of practical training. But, curiously enough, few studies have been made. Several elements, both theoretical and concrete, do stand out and merit examination. The first of these is the psychological commonplace that some stress can foster learning, but that a point can be reached at which the degree of stress becomes immobilizing.

An example of this can be found in the following situation reported by Father M to his supervisor. Father M responded in a confessional situation with considerable sensitivity to a middle-aged man who was experiencing severe doubts about his own worth as a human being. This led to a request for counseling, and in the first session, in which the focus was on the man's feelings about himself, Father M worked well in helping the man externalize heretofore unexpressed feelings. Father M was taken by the man's plight and prior to the second scheduled session did a considerable amount of reading on the causes for low self-esteem and the way to help an individual with these feelings. He also asked for feedback from his supervisor on the quality of his own interaction with his counselee in order to help the man better. When the time for the session came about he entered into it feeling well prepared to assist the man.

In the second session, the counselee divulged the fact that his doctors were afraid lest he have an incurable illness and he was depressed over this; his invalid wife was dependent on him for financial, emotional and physical support; a teenage son was having difficulties with the law as a result of having been caught with illegal drugs. At this point Father M's anxiety level rose sky-high. He had gone into the session with the expectation that he would be able to help the man and was totally unprepared for the problems that surfaced. He felt unable to help and reported wondering as the man's story unfolded, "My God, now what do I do?" He was unable to come up with any answers. Instead, as he was later able to recognize, he joined with his counselee in a common but equally fruitless process of denial by exploring the possibility of finding new and better doctors. In effect, his inability to cope with this situation led to an active participation in, even an initiation of, the psychological defense mechanism of denial.

Another source of stress is the new priest's unfamiliarity with the emotionally potent priestly role he is assuming. As the priest begins his work he does so using a number of externals as supports. These serve as a bridge between himself and those with whom he works. These externals are the signs, duties, and rights of the priesthood. Initially, he does not present himself to his people primarily in light of who he is as a private person, but within the context of the priestly and public role. This role covers and colors his own person because it is public and one of importance and of use to those who rely on the Church and its priests. Because of the way this role functions in his initial pastoral relationships, his own ability to relate to others, an ability which involves the more personal elements in his character, is not put to the test in the very beginning. Rather, he begins by utilizing the institutional strengths of a role. This in itself is sufficiently new to cause anxiety. He has the liturgy in which he functions in a ritualized way. He has the normative and paternal aspects of his pastoral office. He has the theology of the Church which defines and values his priesthood and which gives him an authority as he functions in that role.

The existence of this role and the work he does within its confines give him a buffer in his relationships with people. The role allows for distance in relationships in a way that is not always common in other professional situations. Whether this distance is helpful to him or not depends on his need for distance or closeness, and whether it makes for effective or ineffective pastoral work depends on the way in which he uses it. The point to be noted here is that, helpful or harmful, distance is a reality and looms large in his initial pastoral efforts. Further, the role and the distance are new, they are unfamiliar and they require new ways of relating, and this is the making of a stressful situation.

To understand the significance of this initial reliance on a role, we can contrast the beginning situation of the priest with that of other professionals whose training focuses less on externals and more on their ability to relate personally with those whom they are helping, as is the case with the counselor or the clinical psychologist. They work directly and in a non-mediated way with their clients. The nature of their work requires that the prime medium for help be the relationship itself. Their emotions, failings, strengths, and their own needs are more directly involved with their clientele. From the very beginning of their work, who they are as individuals is on the line. They do not have externals like the Roman collar and vestments of the priest and the rites of the Sacraments, or the white coat of the doctor and the rituals associated with hospital testing and medical examinations.

It would be a serious mistake to assume that either the closeness of personal interaction or the distance of a ritualized relationship is more helpful to the beginning priest. Not only does this depend on the needs of the particular situation itself, but on the personality of the individual priest as well. The human need for distance and closeness varies with each individual and can be described in different ways. One useful description is that of the noted psychologist Karen Horney who makes a threefold distinction: dependence or compliance, which is a function of moving toward people; detachment or withdrawal, which can be seen as moving from people; aggression, which is moving against people. (*Our Inner Conflicts*, New York; Norton, 1945) But no matter how we describe the manner in which the needs for closeness or distance enter into the personality of any individual, we must recognize these needs for the realities they are. They will surface visibly in the work of the beginning priest in surroundings sufficiently unfamiliar to produce some anxiety.

Pastoral work surfaces one of the flaws in seminary training. The seminarian has been trained to fit in and to put up with things more than to respond in adaptive and creative ways or to change things. Seminary training does not equip him well to deal with pastoral crises and emergency situations. He has learned a pattern of responses in the seminary, but they are responses merely for coping with the rather singular demands of seminary life. Faced with the need for a positive and direct response and quick action to assume control of a situation, the young priest often finds himself at a loss. He has learned how to fit in and put up with things, and how to cope with situations in which other people are in charge. Now the responsibility for designing a response is his. This he has not yet learned to do. Placed in a situation in which the demands are more secular, the beginning priest on occasion will revert to a pattern of coping which was established prior to his seminary years.

We can also anticipate that at moments of stress his ability to adapt his behavior to the needs of the situation will decrease, not increase. Noting this same point with reference to the training of medical students, a group of medical educators makes the following point: "It should be emphasized that *all* people have preferred modes of behavior, and that with exaggeration of the stress component of a situation, they are likely to adhere more rigidly to these trends, despite the fact that greater flexibility is the more adaptive and appropriate response." (*Teaching and Learning in Medical School,* George Miller, ed. Cambridge: Harvard, 1961) This is equally true of the beginning priest. In the seminary he was schooled in theological responses to crisis situations, but he has not been exposed to those crises in which his responses can be put to the test. As a result, when he confronts crises in his beginning work, it is often for the first time. The chief strengths that he brings to bear during moments of pressure are not the strengths of the priesthood, because he has not yet had the opportunity to interiorize these strengths through the human process of living with them. Rather, he falls back on his own personal and probably unprofessional way of coping with crisis. This may have worked in his earlier private life, but it proves inadequate for the pastoral situation, as the following incident points out.

Father O joined a group of young clergy who met weekly for recreation and to discuss common concerns. The group was structured, had an elected chairman, and a system for delegating responsibility. Their meeting facilities were uncomfortable and frequently the butt of jokes. Faced with bad facilities, Father O went ahead on his own and arranged for better ones in a more centrally located parish whose clergy did not participate in the group. He then informed the group of the change, which they accepted without comment. On one occasion, the new host pastor, faced with a conflicting schedule for the use of the meeting room, expressed some annoyance at Father O because of the clergy group's presence in his parish. Father O felt embarrassed by the pastor's public criticism. He also expected the members of the group to support him and expressed some anger at them when they looked on the incident as his problem, not theirs. Looking into this incident with his supervisor, Father O noted that his behavior was part of a common pattern. As the oldest of several children, he had always charged ahead when something needed doing. He would then expect support from his younger brothers and would get quite angry at them if the support were not forthcoming. As the oldest and biggest, he was usually able to whip them into shape. In the situation described above, and as he came to see in many others, he was reverting to the old manner. A crisis had come up and he had charged ahead to resolve it. But by so doing he had stepped outside the group's decision-making processes and assumed an authority that was properly the group's. Not that they were unhappy at this; on the contrary, they were content to have him take the responsibility for finding a better and more convenient meeting room. But because they hadn't asked him to do this, since he had acted unilaterally, they also let him have the blame.

Although seemingly trivial, this incident was troubling. Father O was publicly embarrassed by a senior pastor and felt abandoned by his peers. It was helpful for him to understand that his peers had not violated any unwritten agreement in not supporting him. He, on his own, had worked himself into an unworkable situation. And he had done so by reverting to an old problem-solving pattern that was no longer useful.

Although the priest, like the doctor, begins his work with the utilization of externals, sooner or late, if his work is to be effective, he will also have to initiate the sort of helping relationship in which who he is as a person is on the line. When he deals with a bereaved husband, or the layman who finds no consolation in religious practices, or the individual who with terror is facing death and finds religious rites not helpful—at this point when either the externals do not help or he does not know how to use them, his own individual and personal resources become critical. Also, at this point, the level of his anxiety can be expected to go high, and he will revert to his preferred mode of behavior. This can be a source of difficulty because here, too, his preferred mode of behavior and his personal resources may not be useful, and in all likelihood have not been put to the test in crisis situations typical in pastoral work.

Another anxiety-producing circumstance for the beginning priest is the fact that he is beginning. In and of itself, getting started is difficult, sufficiently difficult to cause real stress. As he begins, the new priest has realized what has been a chief goal for many years, ordination, and now is on the threshold of living the life of the priest. For some, ordination itself may be the goal. Father R, having for many years set his heart on being ordained a priest, noted that the period after ordination was surprisingly difficult. He had seen ordination as the culmination, not the beginning, and found that after ordination he was expected to go to work. For most, ordination is both culmination and beginning. They have looked forward to the beginning of their priestly work and now it is within their grasp. The normal difficulties experienced by a beginner loom large for the beginning priest because the expectations placed on him are so high. And that which threatens or appears to threaten this long-sought goal will be a source of considerable anxiety.

Beginning difficulties often strike a familiar note. One difficulty which the priest had hoped would be a part of his past—the feeling of helplessness (which we will examine in greater detail later in this chapter)—proves to be especially frustrating. As a seminarian, not only was he at the mercy of his teachers for the grades he would receive, but, more than other professional students, he was subjected to a scrutiny, evaluation, and judgment about his fitness for ordination. In all this he was an interested but impotent onlooker. To experience this frustration as he starts his priestly work, to be so terribly dependent on the good will or assistance of the pastor, secretary, janitor, school principal, or other significant people is an unpleasant surprise. This, too, will raise the level of anxiety.

Equally important is the objective difficulty of many ordinary pastoral situations. It is common for the new man to be exposed to a variety of situations which, because of their difficulty, are usually the province of specialists. The beginning priest can be seen by those seeking his help as one of these specialists, but he usually doesn't feel like one. Rather, he frequently feels overwhelmed by the scope and variety of the situation brought to him. Father L reported that in one afternoon shortly after his arrival he had to make funeral arrangements for a parishioner and comfort the survivors, try to counsel by telephone a suicidal woman, and give the last rites to and anoint a man who had been badly mangled in an automobile accident. He said that he went in to dinner so emotionally drained that he couldn't eat. Father M said that within two weeks of his arrival he had to cope with the pregnancy of a young parish girl and didn't know what to do. Father J reported that his first contact was with a con man. "I knew he was a con artist, but I never had to deal with one before. I didn't know what to do. He so flustered me that I was tied up in knots in two minutes." Father B, working in a poor parish, noted that many people who came to him lived in worlds filled with pain and despair. Although he thought he should want to help them, he responded, "I can't wait to get out of their world," and felt very guilty about his attitude. Father C reported that "things are coming much faster than I had expected" and felt overwhelmed. Father D summed it up, "Every time I turn around there are people wanting something, and the needs are so obvious. People need so much help. All I seem to confront are situations that call for help." The work is demanding, the needs are real, and the variety almost limitless. Moving into this situation, the new priest can be expected to experience considerable stress and anxiety.

The beginner often brings into particularly irksome situations the anxiety he experiences in getting started. He will blame people or attack situations as a way of coping with his anxiety when it would be more productive to see his anxiety as an inevitable part of starting out. Father T, assigned to the staff of a campus ministry, arrived before the man he was replacing left. Thus he had no office of his own. It was clear that the office would be vacated in six weeks, but the lack of an office in the beginning became the focal point for a real crisis. Appointments could not be made because he had no place where he could see people. Work was not getting done because he needed a place to work and didn't have one. It became obvious that the office was the symbol of the difficulties Father T was having in getting started. As he said at one point, "If I don't get settled in soon, I don't know what's going to happen. I don't know what I'll do." He had a real need to "get settled in," but not just into an office. The process of getting started was taking time, more time than he could tolerate comfortably. Much like the new students on his campus, he was finding it hard to get to know people, to make friends, and to find ways to do his work. But unlike the students, he had worked and waited for many years for this moment, the stakes were very high, and he found the delays not only frustrating but positively frightening.

If we examine the comments made by a number of priests during their beginning months, one common theme stands out—the challenge is frightening. It is a time of real challenge which is sufficiently strong that it threatens to overwhelm the individual. It is common for the beginning priests to report that they do not know what to do in given situations, and this is frightening. This fear or state of fright, which we have referred to elsewhere as "beginners panic," is a real crisis. The label indicates that it is one of those initial worries at which the initiate will someday look back with fond amusement. For those who succeed this may well be the case. It is a true crisis, however, in that the individual's ideas, self-image, and coping mechanisms are put to the test, and found wanting. He confronts a situation which points out, quite forcefully, that who he is and what he has to offer are not adequate to the demands of the situation. This precipitates feelings of self-doubt and inadequacy, questions about whether he has what it takes, and, on occasion, whether or not the decision for the priesthood was a mistake.

In addition, it is common to fear that the particular assignment is not a workable one, as the following example illustrates. Several weeks into his hospital chaplaincy, Father K found himself feeling angry toward the medical and nursing staff at the hospital. On several occasions he was tempted to make comments about the insensitivity of the doctors and the mechanical attitudes of the nurses. He noted that patients were well cared for physically but "that the human dimension is being overlooked." He wondered whether it was possible for a priest to function in such a context. Father L, after several weeks in his new parish, began to wonder whether they really needed a young priest there. He saw most of the priests working with older people. It seemed that most of the parishioners already had satisfying pastoral relationships with the other priests, and there didn't seem to be all that much work to do. Father D, in a similar situation, reported that very few people came to the rectory for help and that "all the other things you can do are already someone else's responsibility, and they don't want you butting in." These examples could be multiplied many times. In each of the cases, the feeling tone of the situation was much the same—discomfort often moving into frustration and sometimes anger, and a general sense of foreboding, the fear lest the assignment not work out.

In each of these situations, the issue was resolved and the resolution focused around two points: people to work with and a sense of pastoral competence. The question of a clientele, or people to work with, is a critical issue. To do well and make a success of his work, the new priest needs people with whom and for whom he can work. The possibility that there might not be anyone or enough people who want his assistance is frightening. This fear surfaces quite frequently and, as in the above examples, right when he is trying to settle into his new assignment. It doesn't take a long time to bring this fear to the panic point. A few days spent in the rectory alone waiting for the telephone or the doorbell to ring while the other more established priests are busy about their work often proves sufficient. Even situations like visitations at hospitals, where the clientele is guaranteed, can be stressful. The beginning priest might not know how to go about starting a conversation with a patient. Father K, mentioned above, had experience visiting sick people, but not as a priest. While a seminarian he had visited the sick but had assumed that most serious matters should be discussed in the context of the Sacrament of Penance, or with a priest "who can do something about them." Now that he was ordained, he was frightened at the prospect of having to deal with issues that once he could refer to the chaplain. Although in a certain sense he did have a ready-made clientele, he did not have easy access to this clientele. It was up to him to create that access by becoming comfortable with his new role. This he found very difficult.

The question of adequate skills is equally large. Often at the heart of hesitancy to get involved in a pastoral situation lies the fear that the individual will not be able to cope with it. This is an obvious part of the fear expressed by Father K in this example. In most of these instances, confidence came with repeated exposure to people, difficult and stressful though this exposure may have been. The beginner's panic was reduced as the beginner overcame initial shyness, as his presence became more noted, and as some initial successes buttressed confidence in his abilities.

Not all instances of beginner's panic are so easily resolved. In the following situation the beginning priest had to make a shift in his work. Father W was working in a parish which had a long tradition of high visibility on the part of the clergy. The people were accustomed to bringing their parish priests into all aspects of their lives. Initial fears that he did not have the resources to cope with considerable human interaction proved true.

Father W first reported that he enjoyed working with his people, but within one month of his arrival he was feeling the pressure. He noted that he "enjoyed working very much but there is the pressure of the work all the time, and too much work," so that he is "not enjoying it now." He wanted to know whether this was a problem merely for him or whether this is a problem for all priests. Father W found it comforting to learn that his reaction was not all that uncommon. However, the pressure continued and several weeks later he reported that it was beginning to overwhelm him. "Every place I go, I see people in need. I have no place where I am able to get away from it."

At this point, with the pressure of demand very heavy on him, he began to wonder whether or not he had the ability to meet the demands of parochial work. "I think I have had one too many experiences of disillusionment and I'm beginning to feel like I don't have the energy for being wiped out anymore. I just want to go away and become anonymous and help people within the limits of my abilities without being overwhelmed by the magnitude of all the demands." Sometime later, he recognized that the demands of parochial life were more than he could cope with. "I feel like I would like to quit. I'm in charge and I don't want to be in charge. I have never wanted to be in charge, so I quit." Recognizing that his reactions were a valid estimate of his strengths, he requested and received a transfer to a more structured and secluded administrative position.

This beginner's panic is a common experience. As with many troubling situations, putting a label on it is a first and useful step in reducing it to manageable proportions. Peer support and the direct knowledge that his peers are going through the same thing in their own work setting also proves helpful. It depersonalizes the difficulty and emphasizes the structural quality of it. Nonetheless, it is real; it is genuinely stressful and it is crucial because it deals with initial feelings about the appropriateness of his vocational choice. Handled well it can be constructive. Left to deal with this alone the beginning priest will probably find it a scarring experience.

Another affecting element in the beginning priest's situation is his need to work out an identification with the priestly role. We have already looked at this with regard to the several options that present themselves to him, and now we will look at this as an anxiety-related process. It is a psychological commonplace that the passage from adolescence to adulthood is a time of stress. The ease or difficulty that marks the process will affect its success, and the success is going to affect the individual's ability to function as an adult.

In addition to ages which typify both adolescence and adult patterns, there are roles which can be seen as specifically adult roles or as specifically adolescent roles. These roles shape the responses and attitudes of the individuals who function within them. Further, they do not necessarily take into account the maturity or lack of maturity of the individual. For instance, the role of a student is a dependent role. He is in a position subordinate to that of the teacher. What he knows is not valued as much as what the teacher knows, and his abilities are still in the process of being proven. He is relating to an educational system that will decide whether or not to put its stamp of approval on him. By its nature, this role is a subordinate one, analogous to adolescence.

A newly ordained man who is making the transition from the role of a seminarian to that of a priest is making a transition from a subordinate role, one typified by the status and expectations associated with adolescence, to a role that is typified by the expectations associated with an adult. Further, these qualities attach themselves to the role independently of the individual's own situation. To be a seminarian and a student is to be in a role that by definition is incomplete. It is the process of moving toward full maturity. To be in the role of a priest, by reason of the nature of the role itself and independent of the individual who bears the role, presupposes that this goal has been attained. The time spent moving from the one role to a state of comfort within the other is as difficult on the professional level as it is for the individual actually moving from adolescence to adulthood. The fact that a priest might have already made this move in his personal life does not mean that he will be exempt from having to make it in his priestly life. He might know what it feels like as an individual to be an adult, but he does not know yet what it feels like to function as a priest in an adult manner. This he must go through experientially.

An example of this is the stress he experiences as he learns to relate to the public and visible dimension of his role. In the work that he does, he is being sought out because of his public identity. Were he an unordained layman he would not be sought out. He is presenting himself and is being sought out as a public representative of the Church. The people with whom he works have already had experiences with the Church. They bring these experiences and all the expectations that go with them to the newly ordained priest and presuppose a continuity from the other clergy to this new one. Those who are relating to the new priest are coming to him first because of this public role. In a very real sense he is an official of the Church. His personality emerges only subsequently.

For the newly ordained priest this is usually not the way it seems. His previous experience is that of an individual, not a public figure. He does not usually feel a sense of continuity with all the Church representatives with whom these people have dealt. His relationships prior to this have been mostly personal and not public. To have the laity vent on him their anger for the actions of clergy whom he has never met and who may even have died before he was born is a puzzling experience. He does not sense any continuity between other clergy and himself. To him, it feels like a personal attack and often is experienced as being as unpleasant as it is puzzling. It is difficult for him to learn how to recognize the validity of the feelings that are expressed by these people, that as an individual he is not responsible for them, but that as a representative of the Church he must deal with them as the realities they are.

Not only are these feelings a nuisance to the priest, but they are an obstacle to the people in their life in the Church. The feelings get in the way of a mature relationship with the Church. The new priest can help the people by teaching them to claim responsibility for their own feelings the way an adult must. But teaching others to respond in an adult way is usually as new and difficult a task as it is important. The fact that he has made the transition from adolescence to adulthood in his own life will assist him in this, but it does not substitute for it. He must make the very same transition from the adolescent role, that of a student, to the adult role, that of a public and visible priest. The following example can serve to illustrate the difficulties presented here.

Father J, a man in his mid-thirties, entered the seminary after several years in a profession for which he had received professional training on the graduate school level. He was a man of obvious ability, intelligence, and talent. These proven abilities did not exempt him from the need to move into the priestly role by going through the same process of adaptation and growth required of much younger and less accomplished individuals. Typically, his entry into his pastoral work was beset by difficulties that confront the beginner. Given charge of two important parish groups, he questioned the effectiveness of his work. He did not see any real success marking his efforts. Although his new pastoral relationships were with lay people who had no official status, he said that he did not feel as though he were on an equal footing with these people. Similarly, he did not know how he fit in with the parish staff.

When his supervisor pointed out to him that he was "a quiet but effective pacesetter on the staff," he was "rather taken aback by this." However, the supervisor pointed out to him that he had "suggested staff meetings and that they were now having them," and he had suggested "working out schedules ahead of time and this was being done, and that these are both significant items in any parish." Also, he noted that the parish groups that the new priest was directing were moving slowly into organized and self-sustaining bodies.

What is going on here is that the personal strengths of Father J are surfacing in his work. But it did not feel to him as though this were the case. He felt very much the unskilled beginner. He did not know how to use this new authority that was his. In short, he had taken on a new and significant role and had not yet learned to relate to this role and felt uncomfortable in it.

Another real source of stress is that as part of his daily life the new priest frequently has to cope with human situations that the average person meets only rarely. Serious or terminal illness, death and all the involvement associated with funerals, family problems and marital dissolution, unemployment, and other aspects of social insecurity are troubles which obviously do not enter into the average individual's life with frequency. These are crises, and we have developed a number of social and emotional means to help people cope with these crises lest they prove overwhelming.

One of the means for coping with them is the assistance of the clergy. Whether in ritualized ways, as with funerals, or in direct and more personal ways, as in counseling situations, the priest is called on to help at these difficult times. Thus the beginning priest has to deal with these situations from the very beginning and with some frequency. What are for other people times of crisis are for him part of his regular pastoral duties.

The experience of stress and anxiety in initial pastoral contacts and the need to cope with crises and the unexpected has several effects on the priest as he begins his work. He is surprised by the difficulty of coping with pastoral situations and notes that what he learned in his seminary years does not seem immediately helpful. As a result, he can end up dismissing their education, often in anger.

Others may feel overwhelmed and threatened by these crises and retreat from them. This retreat is not necessarily a precipitous flight, but more commonly involves the development of a sense of apprehension relative to these situations, an ability to anticipate them, and the development of some mechanism that allows them to be avoided. With the avoidance of them, however, comes an avoidance of the people in the situations. As will be noted later, this initiates one of the more destructive patterns of coping, a movement toward isolation.

For these several reasons, the beginning priest finds anxiety and stress to be normal accompaniments to his pastoral efforts. He is making a major institutional transition from the seminary to a pastoral setting. He is making a major change in role from that of a student to that of a professional. He is moving into a highly visible role about which most people frequently have strong feelings. He is, from the beginning, asked to deal with situations against which most people try to guard themselves, such as illness, death, and social disruption. And finally, to make it even more difficult, he is expected to do this generously and competently. Because of the objective difficulty of his situation, learning how to adapt to the life and demands of the priesthood as he must live it will be a source of anxiety and stress for the beginning priest.

In summary, then we can note that stress and anxiety are normal accompaniments of the beginning period of pastoral work. There is much that of necessity is new, the work is difficult, and the desire for success high and the possibility for failure quite real. Further, this stress and anxiety usually come as a surprise and often throw the new man into a state of panic. In his response to the anxiety and pressure, he can be expected to revert to older, more accustomed ways of coping, ways which are frequently less suited to the demands of the situation. Also, stress and anxiety can immobilize the abilities of the new man.

The Intimacy Crisis

It is in the context of this stressful situation that the beginning priest must resolve the crises that are part of his life. At the beginning of this chapter we mentioned three crises that are particularly functional and significant in the life of the beginning priest. We will now look into each of these beginning with the intimacy-identity crisis.

Earlier we spoke of the task of establishing a pastoral identity. Often this was spoken of not as a task but a crisis. Much has been written about identity-crisis in the life of the clergy. Erik Erikson, who originated the notion in *Identity, Youth and Crisis* (New York: Norton, 1968, p. 16), comments, that "everybody has heard of 'identity-crisis' and it arouses a mixture of curiosity, mirth and discomfort which yet promises, by the very play on the word 'crisis', not to turn out to be something as fatal as it sounds."

While this comment is well taken, and the caution that we understand crisis to be a pivotal situation and not a disaster especially important, the fact remains that the concept of identity is useful. Erikson cites an example of what he means by identity in the letter of William James: "A man's character is discernable in the mental or moral attitude which, when it came upon him, he felt himself most deeply and intensely active and alive. At such moments there is a voice inside which speaks and say: '*This* is the real me.' " (Ibid., p. 19) In this example we can see that sense of self which bespeaks who a person is, his identity.

An experience which would send the individual reeling and remove that sense of comfort and assuredness in who he is could well be considered an attack on that sense of self. It would well precipitate the critical situation described as an identity-crisis. This is not the experience reported by our beginning priests. Difficult situations are reported as being difficult, not personally shattering. Some pastoral experiences may be unpleasant, and the beginning priest may dislike this unpleasantness, but he usually comes through them with his sense of self intact. Even the difficult task of adjusting to and incorporating a new role, the public identity of the priest, does not overwhelm the individual's sense of self. A possible explanation for this situation is that the seminary years provide the opportunity for both a moratorium from demands of growth and a supportive context for firming up gains already made. Whatever the cause, the beginning priests begin their work with an apparently well-grounded sense of personal identity.

This does not mean that the initial period is free from crises. Our experience has been that there is, indeed, a major crisis in the life of the beginning priest. This crisis proves to be the overriding issue in the life of the priest as he begins his work. The other tasks and other crises he must face—the need to become an insider, the need to work out a pastoral identity, the need to develop an analytic and professional sense, and the ability to cope with the disillusionment and sense of letdown that often comes after about six months of priestly work—all become more clearly focused through this key issue. This is the intimacy crisis. Briefly put, this intimacy crisis concerns the need to establish human relationships that are both personally satisfying and professionally productive. Compared with this need, all others become secondary. The truly threatening problems that come up during this period of entry into pastoral work prove to be intimacy issues. In contradistinction to questions of identity, these intimacy issues do raise potentially critical questions. The intimacy issues usually focus on questions of relationships, carrying personal expectations from the working to the living situation and vice-versa, and the need to establish an appropriate distance and closeness in all situations.

In an article that is both incisive and insightful, Dr. Kenneth

Mitchell addresses the intimacy issue. ("Priestly Celibacy from a Psychological Perspective" *The Journal of Pastoral Care,* vol. 24, Dec. 1970, pp. 216ff.) Also using the categories of Erik Erikson he notes that the development of a sense of identity is usually accomplished in the early twenties and that the issues which surface the intimacy crisis do not arise until after the decision is made for ordination. This observation is helpful in understanding the dynamics of transition from seminary life to that of the priesthood. We would like to complement this view with another perspective.

When a priest begins his pastoral ministry, several elements enter into his life. First, he is a much more visible individual than he was as a seminarian. As we have noted, he has become a public figure. He is given supports for this new role, but they are role supports and very different from supports given a seminarian. As a seminarian he had a ready-made peer group for support. He had counselors to whom he could turn, friends with whom he could recreate, and, all in all, a group of people who had come to know and learn how to cope with him, his personality, his eccentricities, and his way of relating. Without denying either the demands of seminary life, the filtering process that takes place in the seminary, or the competition among the seminarians, it is still true that the seminary provides the type of support that makes these pressures tolerable. The life structure generally provides the possibility of comfortable and undemanding relationships with like-minded people of an equal status.

In beginning his pastoral ministry, the young priest finds a radical shift taking place in the area of relationship. To begin with, he is moving from a community with a large number of people, much like a college fraternity, to a living situation where there are usually only a small handful of people. This transition is a difficult one, as can be illustrated in the following description of a young priest arriving at his first assignment. Father M reported that when he first arrived at St. Michael's Church, there was no one there to greet him. Finally, the custodian let him in but no one was in the house. He noted that the experience was one of considerable loneliness for the house was mostly empty during his first week there. While this description focuses almost exclusively on the sense of loneliness and does not bring in the feelings of excitement that many people anticipate in similar situations, it does underscore the fact that there is a change and that the change is difficult. The difficulty in the change focuses most clearly on the area of relationships. Within these relationships the beginning priest is looking for certain things, and what it is he is looking for is knit together by what Erikson calls intimacy. He is looking for relationships in which he will experience appreciation, support, a sense of his own self-worth, and a sense of belonging.

The intimacy issue gives shape to other issues. The other tasks and challenge end up being translated into relational terms. The beginning priest who is having a difficulty becoming an insider does not experience difficulty in the process of entry. What he experiences is the fear that they don't need him, or that they don't like him and don't want him. The priest who is having difficulty working out a role identification in which he is comfortable experiences a lack of relationship, a feeling of helplessness, and worries about what he can do for people. The priest who is struggling with the need to work out contracts can experience personal frustration in trying very hard and seeing his best efforts miss the mark. He will doubt his ability to fit in, to relate to people, and to be a part of them. He has gone through this in his adjustment to seminary life, but at that time he knew that the seminary was temporary. Now he is in it for real and the stakes are much higher.

In order to see the elements of the intimacy crisis more concretely we will look at three typical areas in which it surfaces: the relationship between the working and living situation, over-involvement, and isolation or under-involvement. We will begin with the living situation.

The relationship of the new priest's working situation to his living situation is a source of considerable turmoil. It is a source of turmoil because the new priest is placed in a situation that is objectively quite difficult. It is especially troubling because the objective difficulty is frequently unarticulated and passed over. To understand the difficulty and the turmoil it causes we will draw on the ideas of Erving Goffman (in his book, *Asylums*. New York; doubleday Anchor, 1961) who describes the essential characteristics of what he calls a total institution. These characteristics apply at least analogously to the situation of the new priest. Among these is the fact that those involved in total institutions live and work together. This is such a commonplace characteristic in priestly and religious life that it would not even be worth the notice were it not for the fact that almost all the rest of the world carefully separates living and working from each other. Many of the young priest's friends, relatives, and parishioners will spend a portion of their day commuting to and from work, and will do this in order to keep the two separated. The fusion of the two, which they do not want, is the lot of the priest.

Keeping working and living separated is important because the average individual has a definite set of expectations, be they conscious or subconscious, of his working situations. He has another set of expectations of his family or living group. Survival, to say nothing of well-being, usually requires that the expectations be distinct. What a man expects of his employer and co-workers and what he expects of his wife and children are ordinarily quite different. Work relationships and love relationships are not the same.

What a man expects from his work and what he expects from his family are sufficiently important to our purpose that they are worth noting. It is helpful to begin by looking at the usual source of these expectations, family life. Noting that every man has not one but several families, Ackerman distinguishes the family of childhood, the family of marriage and parenthood, and the family of grandparenthood (in *The Psychodynamics of Family life*. New York: Basic Books, 1958, p. 17). For the sake of simplicity we will call the family of childhood the primary family and the family of marriage and parenthood the secondary family. In addition, following Mitchell, we can speak of a tertiary family. This is not a family in the true sense because it refers to the working situation, and, as we have noted, work and family relationships are different. But because of the significance that work and working relationships have to many people, second only to their family, we can examine work relationships relative to family relationships at least in order to point out the differences.

It may not be appropriate to speak of expectations in the primary family since the individual may be too young to understand what this means. However, we can point out the qualities in the family with regard to childhood and note the effect they have on shaping adult expectations. These are quite fundamental such as protection, education, nurturing, affection, and support in a very broad way. The young individual is quite dependent on the good will of his elders; the degree to which they respond to his basic needs will affect his later life. This is such commonplace knowledge that we shall pass over it to those areas more relevant to our subject, the secondary and tertiary families. The expectations an individual has of his secondary family are more in the order of closeness and sexual intimacy, personal affection, and personal valuing. It is also true that an individual may want the status that goes with the married state, and the security that goes with a permanent relationship. From the tertiary family, in addition to his salary, the individual will be looking for a means for gaining status and position in the eyes of those important to him, an area for achieving success and giving reign to his ambitions, and the establishment of some area in which he is in control. These relationships are usually more distant than those in the family. Working for higher position and success, which often entails control of others, is legitimate in a working situation where it is generally understood that the relationships are utilitarian. Personal friendships, affection, and socializing are secondary goals, if, in fact, they are goals at all. When they become primary goals, as sometimes happens, in which the employees' socializing and friendships become more important than getting the work done, a crackdown by the person in charge is usually needed.

In a family this same competition, aggressiveness, or utilitarian approach, an approach which is legitimate in business, becomes destructive. The relationships in the family and at work differ in the kind of gratification that can be expected from each, in the degree of closeness in each, in the scope of the relationship, and in the area of permanence and security.

This description of work and family life does not describe the situation of the priest, for his situation is different for two reasons. First, he has no true secondary family. Second, what passes for his secondary family, the rectory, and his tertiary family, the working situation, are ordinarily combined. This makes for an extraordinary and often overwhelming mixing of different and even conflicting expectations. His desires for closeness, affection, personal support, and the need for relaxation are focused ordinarily on the same group in which he will exercise his ambition, his desire for advancement and success, and his hopes for status and prestige. Affection and personal support bespeak a relationship marked by some closeness and intimacy. Competition for position and success bespeak limited personal involvement and greater distance. To look for both this distance and closeness at the same time with the same group will obviously create conflict. And yet this is the situation of the average priest as he begins his pastoral work.

To make this more explicit and concrete we will use the following examples. Father J, a member of a religious order, was assigned to a parish staffed by his order. After many years in a seminary he experienced as "impersonal," he was looking forward to a more familial and personal way of living. In addition, in looking at his future work, he hoped to be able to work corporately with the other members of the parish staff in team ministry. To him, team ministry meant periodic staff meetings, corporate decision-making, and keeping each other very much informed about what each individual on the staff was doing.

At Father J's request the pastor scheduled a staff meeting. Prior to this meeting most communication had taken place informally or by means of notes from the pastor. At the meeting Father J expressed his hope that they would be able to work together and spoke of some of his own hopes for the parish. The other staff members, unaccustomed to these meetings, appeared ill at ease and were silent. He noted that the silence and discomfort often carried over into the dining room and invaded the moments the priests were together for social activities. Obviously something was wrong, and Father J interpreted it as a negative reaction to his hopes and an unwillingness to change anything. The situation did not change, staff meetings became semi-silent struggles for control and the living situation more tense.

In analyzing the situation and evaluating Father J's role in it, several facts surfaced. First, the introduction of this staff meeting changed or threatened to change staff relationships in a way that proved uncomfortable for the staff members. Heretofore, the informal and casual way of communicating had allowed each man an area of responsibility in which he could do what he chose. He had his area, his turf, and by unwritten agreement no one would intrude on his turf. Father J's request for information about each man's activity, well-intentioned though it may have been, was an intrusion on his turf. At least implicitly, it was calling him to account for what he was doing there. The response on the part of the other priests on the staff to his ideas and requests was an attempt to preserve distance in work relationships. Each was working competently and well and had little to fear from a possible review of his work. Nor had they much to fear from a new man, especially one fresh from the seminary, who was not in a position to question their competence. However, they did have much to fear from someone who would change the system in a way which would require that the distance in their working relationships be changed. Because of the identification of the secondary family with the working staff, and the carryover from working to living situation, the staff controlled its working relationships in order to make the living situation tolerable. There was an easygoing and offhand but uninvolved relationship in the rectory which served more as a home base and refuge for the staff than it did as a place in which they worked. Work was done in the church, in the parish offices, and in the local community. It was not brought into the living areas of the rectory, nor did it enter into the relationships among the staff. Father J's proposals threatened to change all this. By introducing staff meetings and work reviews, the distance in work relationships would have been lessened. This would have changed the quality of relationships within the rectory in a way obviously unacceptable to the staff.

It could well be objected here that quality in pastoral work requires team effort and evaluative review by a staff. This is both true and not the point. What we are looking at here is not the quality of pastoral work but the human survival of the pastor. Questions of relationship touch areas that are so fundamental to human life that they can not be taken lightly. In this particular situation the staff had worked out its own way of separating working from living. Implicitly, they were saying that they could not tolerate a complete fusion of the two. The chances are that their instincts leading them to this course of action were correct.

In another situation Fathers K and W, seminary classmates and friends, were assigned to the same large parish. During a meeting of one of the parochial groups, a decision had to be made about a particular course of action. Father W wished to spend some time working toward a consensus. Father K, believing that a consensus would not be possible, pointed out that there was a divergence of opinion and suggested that they go along with the majority view. He noted that "all we're trying to do here is get this job done, and whether we all agree on it or not really isn't very important." Father W reported that he was rather shaken by what he considered to be Father K's businesslike approach to the question. On further investigation it became clear that Father W's basic concern was not with the parochial project but with his relationship with Father K. He was concerned lest a friendship, which was very important to him, turn into a work relationship. The question of the appropriateness or inappropriateness of Father K's remarks was quite secondary to him. What he saw was that a relationship on which he counted for personal support looked as though it might be changing, and such change bothered him.

The stresses inherent in the combination of working and living relationships, and the frequency with which these stresses are overlooked, can be seen in the following situation.

Father T was assigned to a parish whose pastor had been both friend and teacher during Father T's years in the seminary. Both had looked forward to his ordination and had awaited his assignment to the parish.

The pastor had a good reputation among the clergy and in his parish, and took his pastoral duties seriously. He was hard-working, available to his people, and tried to make the Church's theology functional in his parish. It was these good qualities that Father T admired in his friend and pastor. As he moved into his new work in the parish the quality of his relationship with the pastor changed. Tensions began to enter into the previously friendly relationship as the need for quality performance in Father T's work required the pastor to be directive. The older man's suggestions, which were first offered as helpful hints, gradually became more directive and normative. Father T, while not feeling disposed to challenge the objectivity of the pastor's evaluations, was pained by the very fact of the evaluations. The pastor found this equally painful, but decided that his first obligation was to his people, an obligation which required that he see to it that the parish staff maintain a level of quality in their work.

An analysis of the situation revealed several important points. First, both Father T and the pastor had been looking forward to their joint efforts more to meet personal needs than in order to accomplish a set of pastoral goals. The pastor had long looked forward to sharing his efforts with a convivial and supportive companion. He had felt alone in his work and was hoping to gather together a few like-minded individuals whose joint efforts would be mutually rewarding. Whether the desire for this cooperation was primarily personal or pastoral was never articulated. Father T, for his part, wanted to continue working with his friend and saw the separation from the seminary eased by the knowledge that he would be living with a teacher and friend.

Each overlooked the demands of the work relationship. The work relationship was not that of friend to friend or brother to brother, but of pastor to assistant. Put simply, it was an employer-employee relationship. The pastor, a conscientious man intelligent enough to know the difference between good and bad pastoral work, felt obligated to see that his young friend's work lived up to acceptable standards. Father T, equally conscientious, took the suggestions of the pastor to heart. But not only did each take the demands of quality seriously, they also adopted the employer-employee relationship that buttressed and supported these qualitative demands. In doing so, they paid a high price. The easygoing and offhand relationship they had had, in which they could sit and discuss seminary issues or religious matters at length, was gone. Father T found himself seeking out new friends in the parish and the pastor spent more time with his old friends.

This situation proved critical for Father T. He experienced the pastor's attempts at qualitative review of his work as a puzzling rebuff. When the ease in their relationship began to diminish he felt himself at loose ends and rather alone. As the pastor-assistant relationship replaced the friendship relationship, Father T began to feel depressed. These feelings were accompanied by the sense that there was something wrong, and quite possibly with him.

It proved to be quite helpful for Father T to understand what was going on. When he came to see that he and the pastor were wearing too many mutually exclusive hats, he was able to reduce the crisis to manageable proportions. Helped to see that the same two individuals can't be equals (friends) and unequals (employer-employee) at the same time and in the same situation, he had a rationale that helped him make sense of the situation. His need for friends was recognized as strong and valid, as was his desire to be a good and effective priest. The service that his old friend could be to him in helping him be a good priest was also recognized. But the recognition that personal relationships and working relationships each bespeak quite different degrees of distance was of major importance. It helped bring order into an area of personal turmoil.

This question proves to be fundamental for most beginning priests. No matter whether their needs be for support, affection, appreciation, and closeness on the one hand, or autonomy, independence, and distance on the other, we can anticipate that the beginning priest will bring to his work situation needs that are more personal or family issues than work issues. But since he has no family of his own in which to work these out, and since the response to him at the time of his ordination was as much a response to a person as to a priest, he will invariably bring his personal needs into the work situation. The characteristics of an ideal work situation as they are listed by beginning priests bear this out. The emphasis on team ministry, on words like sharing and community, and on community building in its different forms, show concern for elements that go beyond the work situation. These are qualities that are more central in a love relationship than in a work relationship.

It would be a mistake to assume that all beginning priests, or even the average beginner, have a desire for closeness. There are also individuals who wish to be left alone to do their work, who don't want to be bothered by people, and who want any relationships with the laity mediated by their ecclesiastical role. But desire for distance is also a personal and familial expectation put onto the work situation. To assume that every individual wants to establish his own family is incorrect. Some, by choice and temperament, would never do so and they bring to their priestly work the instinct of the bachelor. Further, not only do they bring their instincts but they bring the expectation that their personal desires are appropriate for the working situation. The need to draw a clear distinction between the demands of the working situation and the needs of the individual is as great with the individual who wants distance as with the individual who has a greater need for closeness or intimacy. It also proves just as helpful for the individual to see that he is entitled to his temperament as another individual is.

One theme that is frequently repeated by the beginning priest is the surprise in discovering that the relationships in the rectory are more distant than he had anticipated. For some, this surprise is also a relief. For many others the discovery of distance is not a pleasant surprise. It proves to be a situation about which they have rather strong feelings, namely, feelings of being alone. A fair amount of the beginning priest's energy and attention is focused on these feelings either by way of trying to cope with them or by establishing a situation in which they will change.

Coping with feelings is a conceptually neat phrase, much neater than the reality it bespeaks. Feelings of loneliness can be painful and even overwhelming. Most beginning priests not only experience this loneliness, but also report that they did not expect that they would. Ordination had been a hectic but happy time. It was a time of celebrating and visiting and drawing together classmates and teachers with old friends and relatives. For the family it served as a time of happy reunion. As the newly ordained priest moves into his first assignment, these supports can be stripped away and he finds himself making new friends. During this difficult time, with feelings of loneliness and the fact of being alone either present to him or threatening to become present (and the power of such a threat should not be underestimated), he may well move into one of two typical patterns of action, over-involvement or isolation. Because of the frequency with which this occurs, we will look at each.

Over-involvement can bespeak a loss of the distance that we can expect to find in the relationship between a priest and the people he is serving. This description is not without problems because distance is a word which has negative connotations in pastoral circles. It can mean the cold, uninvolved, uncaring, and insensitive individual. This is not how we use it here. By distance we refer to the limits to a pastoral relationship that are appropriate to and required by the situation. A couple with marriage difficulties, for example, may seek the assistance of their priest. They are asking him to become involved in their relationship to the extent that is necessary to resolve a problem. They are not asking him to become a part of that relationship. To move unbidden into that relationship, to become emotionally involved with the couple in a way which is neither required nor requested, to lose sight of the need to establish and maintain a distance commensurate with the request for help would be a prime example of over-involvement.

In addition, over-involvement can entail taking on too much work. By this we do not refer to the need to learn how to pace oneself, or the frequent situation of the young priest whose enthusiasm leads him to make a number of commitments which become more and more demanding of him. Rather, by over-involvement we are referring to the situation of the beginning priest who is engaged in more personally demanding relationships than either he can cope with or than the situation requires.

In looking at this situation of over-involvement our focus is not as much on the fact of it, as important as this is, but rather on the reason why the beginning priest would be over-involved. Because of the centrality of relationship in over-involvement we can assume that there are personal reasons why this comes about. What is he trying to cope with by this over-involvement? What needs are being met? What stresses, anxieties, or fears lead him into this situation? We will answer these questions by looking at instances of over-involvement as they occur and drawing from them an understanding of it.

Father J was approached by a young woman who wished help in a marriage difficulty. She expressed a sense of being lonely and alone. Her husband, as she put it, "is just hard to talk to." Father J began by meeting with her on a regular basis once a week, and their initial discussions focused on ways in which she could draw out her husband more. With time the focus faded, their discussions became more general, and Father J became more like a confidant than a counselor. He, in turn, began a relationship of providing general religious information and direction for the young woman. The marriage situation remained as an interest and even a problem, but was no longer the central or primary focus. In short, he had become over-involved. This was not only an instance of the type of expansion that can set in with bad contracting, but was a change from a pastoral relationship to a relationship of friendship because of the needs of the individuals involved.

The young woman's loneliness has already been mentioned. She found Father J a kind and responsive person at a time when she was looking for one. He wanted to know whether his years of investment in training for the priesthood were well spent. He wanted to know whether anyone cared about his investment and whether they thought he had anything to offer. Perhaps more than anything else he wished to establish friendship relationships with people in his new parish.

He needed friends for he had left all his old friends behind. The young woman was one of the first people to seek him out and she was a likeable person. The problem, of course, was that the personal relationship was inappropriate in that it was undermining the relationship with her husband.

Over-involvements such as this are common. Requisite distance in pastoral relationships can easily be lost when the pastor, in his own personal life, is looking not for distance but for closeness. It is hard for the beginning priest to switch hats from the personal to the pastoral situation, especially when his living and working combine all of them. Father J was helped to see that he had become over-involved, that the relationship with the young woman was not helping her marriage nor meeting the original request that she brought to him, and that he had a pastoral obligation to help her see that seeking confidants outside her marriage could damage the marriage relationship. He was also helped to recognize the validity of his own need for closeness and for friends. Articulating both the pastoral situation and his own personal needs helped him cope better with his situation. He came to see that discussing his feelings of being alone, his fears of loneliness in his priestly life, and his need for friends were both appropriate and helpful, but that it was not appropriate to do this with a parishioner he was supposed to be counseling. Intellectually, he knew this before he even began. What he didn't know was that he was himself slipping into a situation which he would find inappropriate in others. Granting the need for human relationships and the difficulties of starting in a new parish, it is easy to see how this could happen.

In another situation, Father K became over-involved in his work with a parish commission. A man with high expectations of himself and a need to do well, he was assigned the responsibility for directing this group. The commission was one of a half dozen which met to support and encourage different areas of the parish's life. Its concrete task was important but quite circumscribed and was usually accomplished each year in several three- to four-hour meetings. Father K began to change this. He established monthly meetings which were prepared for with a written agenda mailed out several days prior to each meeting. Voluminous minutes and lengthy reports were prepared and circulated, and a top-heavy bureaucracy was set up. The commission members, responsive to Father K's desire to do well and bemused by the proportions their task was taking, went along with him in the expectation that when his enthusiasm had run its course things would get back to normal.

The members saw an able and enthusiastic new priest and were glad to have him. They did not see how critical and symbolic this task was for Father K. For him the commission held the answer to a number of questions. First among these was the relational question, "Whose priest am I?" The answer was those people addressed in and through the commission. This is an important issue, for while some men may be able to be priests "in general," or exercise their priesthood through specific, short-range tasks such as the regular schedule of weekly Masses, baptisms, confessions, etc., other men have the need to relate to a continuing group of people in many aspects of their lives. This would include all of the above tasks but would go beyond them to include a broader range of personal and familial involvements. This was the case with Father K. In many ways all the preparatory meetings and get-togethers were means to get to know people. They were not needed in order to get the commission's work done, but they were necessary for Father K's subjective and personal needs.

Another question he had was, "Can I succeed?" Again, the answer was centered in the commission and his ability to do a good job there. Doing a good job meant structures, organization, files, and reports. The commission did not need this much work in order to reach its goals. Father K, on the other hand, did need this in order to answer his own subjective questions about his ability to do quality work.

Father K's personal feelings surfaced when one of the commission's members had a baby and asked the pastor to baptize the child. He recognized the woman's right to have the baby baptized by whomever she preferred, yet felt hurt and rejected that he was not asked. He also was troubled both by the strength of the feelings and by what he considered the inappropriateness of his reaction. He, too, had become over-involved and this incident surfaced the over-involvement.

In many ways we can see over-involvement as a symptom. Underneath this symptom there are a number of anxieties and questions which weave together the beginning priest's need for appreciation, support, and friendship. Primary among his anxieties is his need to do well quickly in order to justify many years' investment and a life's work of commitment to a vocation, and usually a lack of experience in coping with questions of closeness and distance. Telling the new priest to slow down, to take things easy, and not to push too hard serves little purpose. This was done with both priests mentioned in these examples, and all it did was raise their level of anxiety. It let them know only that, in addition to being in a discomfort, what they were doing was wrong. An individual who tends to handle his anxieties by becoming over-involved will not be helped. Rather, we may anticipate that he will become more anxious and will handle this anxiety in his usual way of more and more activity, thus making the situation only worse. At times like this, what the beginning priest needs is help in understanding what is going on, why he is doing what he is doing and, most important, an alternative way of proceeding. Understanding coupled with options does not treat just the symptoms but goes effectively to the root cause lying beneath them.

Periodically, the frustrations and problems brought on by over-involvement can lead the beginning priest to withdraw. This isolation need not come only as a flight from over-involvement. It can also be the beginning state of an individual, one who copes with the need to establish an appropriate distance in his working relationships by establishing too great a distance. Isolation, as we use it here, bespeaks a patterned and enduring way of relating. It is not an occasional occurrence, but a state which is marked by greater distance than is required by pastoral needs, and less closeness and involvement than is good for the individual himself. It does not refer only to doing too little work. Rather, it connotes the relational situation of the individual, the fact that in his living and/or working situation there is too little closeness.

In addition to a lack of closeness in the relationships an individual maintains, there is frequently an insufficient number of relationships or pastoral contacts. It is as though the individual finds too many stimuli coming at him too fast, feels in danger of being overwhelmed, and is coping with this apparent assault by keeping the people and the situations at bay. This proves to be a painful situation and is experienced as a defeat.

Father R, assigned to a new parish, arrived and quickly communicated to the people his delight in being there. A personable young man who quickly attracted people to himself, he soon began to discover that his attractiveness brought with it requests for help. He was willing to assist people but the requests were coming faster than he could cope with. Further, the variety of the requests was great. He was asked to assist in the usual round of parish activities and to help in a number of troubled family situations. In addition, he was asked to explain to his rather conservative and structure-oriented people the reasons for changes in the Church. Inevitably this surfaced their dislike of these changes, and the feelings of dislike and unhappiness were directed toward Father R because he was the first priest who was willing to have the people approach him. With time this proved more than he could handle. He began to recognize that many pleasant encounters would eventually get around to discussion of the fact that the Church was changing, and the discussions often became outlets for stored-up, negative feelings. The fact that the people trusted him enough to vent these feelings in his presence, which could objectively be seen as a vote of confidence and an act of trust in him, did not help. To him, they became more in a series of unpleasant encounters and he discovered that he had a very low tolerance for unpleasantness. To ward off this unpleasantness and negativism he began cancelling appointments and generally retreated from public view. Little by little he moved into a state of isolation. The few contacts he had with people were structured and formal and were ended as soon as the business at hand was concluded.

A first look at Father R's state of isolation will highlight the shift from activity to inactivity. However, a second look will show that the major factor at work here was the over-distant quality that became a part of all his relationships. He drew very heavily on the strength of his personality and personal experiences. The distance he established was too great for effective pastoral work, much greater than the people desired, and certainly greater than was good for him. Whereas he initially utilized the role dimension of his new position only partially, he now used only this role, and that very distantly. He knew something was wrong, he did not know what to do about it, and expressed the fear that his whole decision to become a priest was a mistake. His withdrawal into isolation was accompanied by feelings of fear and deep discouragement.

In another situation we can see how the move toward isolation is brought on not by this particular type of scarring experience, but rather by the need to cope with feelings of closeness which proved to be more than the individual could handle. Father S became friendly with a young couple in his new parish. He enjoyed their company and noted how comfortable he felt on the occasions when he visited them. There was some initial confusion about whether they should call him "Father" or call him by his first name, but they eventually called him by his name. With time Father S began to feel uncomfortable in the relationship, not because of any strain or aloofness on the part of his friends but rather from his fear that he might be "using them" as a means to cope with his own feelings of loneliness. Sensitive to the need to serve his parishioners, he wanted to avoid any relationships that could be exploitative. Affective by temperament and with a high need for closeness, and also endowed with enough self-critical ability to understand his motives, he was able to see that the meeting of his own needs played a very significant part in this relationship. Unfortunately, the very real benefit and support that the young couple derived from his friendship did not seem as central to him as his own fears and he progressively saw less and less of them, spending much time alone.

This need to establish an appropriate distance need not result in a traumatic outcome in order to be considered critical. Even in situations of lesser dimension, the issue is important. Father P was approached by a high school classmate shortly after ordination for help with a family problem. He hesitated to answer the request believing that their previous relationship would get in the way of the pastoral relationship. On analysis it became quickly evident that the old friend sought him out in virtue of his priestly role. A counseling relationship was established and maintained drawing on religious structures and the problem was eventually resolved. The issue was minor, but Father P's feelings about it—his initial fears, and then the sense of accomplishment—were very strong. It came as a complete revelation to him that by his actions he could establish a working relationship with his old friend, including establishing a quality of closeness and distance ordered to the goals of the situation. Previously he thought of the distance in a relationship not as something that could be established by thought and choice, but as something which, as he put it, "just happened." That the notion of distance was intelligible, that this distance could be observed in concrete situations, and that distance could be established in chosen situations was both new to him and quite helpful.

Disillusionment

Perhaps one of the most identifiable elements in the intimacy crisis is the period of disillusionment that sets in during the first year. It would be a mistake to write off this disillusionment as post-ordination letdown, assuming it to be a normal and expected occurrence. It is common and can be expected but it is, nonetheless, a true crisis for the individual. The word disillusionment is apt because it bespeaks a process in which the beginning priest's illusions are shot down. They are illusions in the area of relationships. Our experience is that the beginning priests look forward to a success which is measured by the development of personally supportive and professionally satisfying relationships. If these relationships are not established, and if the support and satisfaction are not forthcoming, the effect is traumatic.

Earlier we spoke of the transition from the life of a seminarian to the life of a priest as a radical change in life-style, a change more typical of Eastern than of Western culture. In the process of making this transition the beginning priest must adapt to a very different set of supports and obligations. Put briefly, he is moving from a situation in which he has many personal supports into a situation in which, as a person, he stands alone. The priesthood brings many institutional supports to the individual to assist him in his work, but they are work supports. They are more oriented to helping the individual move into the priestly role and toward supporting him as he exercises that role than they are to meeting his needs as a person. As a seminarian he was part of a peer group of like-minded young men for whom mutual support is typically important. In becoming a priest not only is he singled out as a public and thus somewhat distant person but he is also removed from his supportive group.

One of the especially troubling elements in this situation is that it comes as a surprise. As we pointed out above, the buildup to and celebration of the individual's ordination promises something very different. That the reality should be so different from the expectation is as baffling as it is unpleasant. The new priest anticipates a situation in which the personal quality of his life will remain the same, possibly become more fulfilling. What he experiences, to the contrary, is an affective deprivation. The entry into the new lifestyle proves to be more personally disruptive than anticipated. His illusions about personal supports are negated, and he is disillusioned. This experience of disillusionment is not reflected in the quality of the new priest's work. To look at him from the outside he is competent and productively employed. These crises are interior and private and take place in the lives of well-functioning clergy.

This experience of disillusionment has strong relational components which make it part of the intimacy crisis. We will now look at disillusionment as reported by beginning priests and will draw a schematic interpretation of it based on these experiences. This disillusionment seems to set in about a half year after the new priest begins work, and is accompanied by feelings of depression and letdown. In any event, it is sufficiently troubling, common and critical to merit a description and an attempt at analysis. Typical instances of this depression as reported have a number of elements in common. First, the feelings were strong. One priest reported that he "was feeling really down," another said, "I'm feeling miserable." Asked how things were going, a third said, "Terrible. I'm depressed." What is striking in these feelings is their patterned appearance and predictability. Everyone can have bad days, but it would be a mistake to write these off merely as periodic low moments. The disillusionment crisis is more patterned than that.

Another common element in these examples of letdown and depression is that the individual was not readily able to account for his emotional state. It was not as though something had happened and, as a result, he was feeling depressed. Connecting his subjective state with some event or situation, as with a cause, seems both foreign and difficult. The situation is sufficiently painful and depressing that the individual does not have the reserves of emotional energy to examine his situation. It is at times like this, incidentally, that the view and support of the supervisor is most useful.

Powerlessness

On examination, several causal factors surface. They usually have a strong relational dimension to them. For the sake of structuring our examination we can look at them under the notions of impermanence and powerlessness.

Feelings of impermanence and powerlessness come on the individual unannounced. They come to an individual who, as we pointed out above, by reason of the rite of ordination, the promise inherent in Church structures and, ordinarily, his own expectations anticipated both permanence and power. This is not to say that he sought or preferred power and permanence but, no matter whether he liked them or not, he anticipated they were to be his lot. To experience the opposite, to feel impotent in the face of some challenge or duty and to feel impermanent at the beginning of a life of permanent commitment is an upending experience.

As noted above, the timing for this experience of disillusionment and the feelings of depression, powerlessness, and impermanence that encase this experience can be predicted. In our experience the beginning can be associated with the Christmas holidays. In the common view Christmas is a time of rejoicing and celebration. For many a priest and religious it is a time of loneliness and depression. For the new priest it is especially troubling because it is an experience of a promise which does not come through. Christmas, as we celebrate it in this country, is a time of anticipation and great expectation. There is a big buildup to the day itself and the anticipation that when this day comes there will be a notable sense of fulfillment and personal enjoyment. Preparations for Christmas are ordinarily quite involving. Preparing for the Christmas liturgy, making arrangements for church decorations, involvement in Advent liturgies, and a countless number of large and small tasks in anticipation of Christmas all lead the priest to anticipate that Christmas is quite special. The reality frequently proves to be different. Father L reported that after the last Mass on Christmas morning he locked up the church and went back to the rectory. The older priests had asked to say the earlier Masses and had all left as soon as they were over, precipitously it seemed, for their accustomed concern with the normal duties of a day of public worship disappeared. He spent the rest of the day in an empty rectory becoming progressively more depressed. He noted that "I could have gone out to someone's house but I knew it was a family day and I wasn't part of the family." Father S said that "I never felt so celibate in my life." Father M recalled that as soon as the Christmas morning obligations were taken care of he got in his car and, with another priest, went off for several days of vacation. Father D rather poignantly observed that as he walked around his relatively empty rectory he carried with him a small Christmas present that had been handmade for him by one of his parishioners. In retrospect, he explained this rather singular behavior as some subconscious means of reminding himself that at a time of loneliness people did care for him.

In general, the Christmas season underscores the fact that the new priest does not have his own family. He is a major contributor to and a leading figure in what proves to be a family celebration, but it is as though he were more a catalyst than an active participant in this celebration. Christmas is a family day, the priest plays a central role in setting the stage for this family celebration, but as soon as the familial side of the celebration begins he is no longer a part of it. It is at this point that the distance in his pastoral relationships manifests itself. The lack of intimacy in his life at a time when intimacy is being celebrated, and in many ways Christmas is a celebration of intimacy, is quite painful. All this had been explained to him in his years of seminary preparation but the explanations were often mitigated by the realities of his life. At his ordination this celibate reality again might have been addressed, but the focus of the ceremony was on him in a supportive and enjoyable way. At Christmas, to the contrary, the focus is on his role. The religious side of the Christmas celebration is a ritualized one. It really doesn't matter which priest says the midnight Mass as long as Christmas carols are sung, the liturgy is festive, and the church well decorated with trees and poinsettias.

It is not overstating the fact to say that this concrete realization of what distance is in the life of the celibate priest is traumatic. It is as though his worst fears were being realized. It is from this point that the experience of disillusionment begins to surface.

The Christmas experience appears to have the effect of raising doubts and confirming them. Ordinary human fears of being alone, of not belonging to anyone, of not having a family, and of being painfully different are surfaced and confirmed. How the individual copes with these, of course, is another question. We may anticipate that the usual coping mechanisms, whose extremes are the isolation or over-involvement mentioned above, will come into play.

There is a difference here because this experience also presents the beginning priest with the mobility of his own situation and this proves to be something he cannot cope with easily. He has entered into his first assignment and the questioning brought on by the Christmas experience leads him to recognize that this assignment will not last forever. He is here for awhile but will be moved somewhere else. What he is experiencing is his impermanence.

Father W, a member of a religious order, was very appreciated in the Church agency where he was working. His first pastoral experience had been a positive one as he had thrown himself into his work with enthusiasm and had met with success. After the Christmas holidays it began to sink in that his year's assignment to the agency would come to an end in several months. The prospect of leaving this work and leaving his co-workers with whom he had become quite friendly was painful. In looking ahead to the summer months after leaving the agency, he had strong feelings about not wishing to spend the interim period in any pastoral work prior to beginning his next assignment in September because, as he put it, "I just can't take these temporary relationships."

Father L adverted to the equally temporary quality of his situation and admitted that he did not know how to cope with it. His relationships with the other priests in his parish had become strained over a minor issue and he was afraid that he was not going to have enough time to work out the situation. Further, the problem area was not the strained relationship, for he had managed such situations before, but the need to uproot himself, to leave people behind him, and to go away with issues and relationships left hanging in the air. Another priest, Father P, expressed the fear that he was going to spend the rest of his life getting to know people, "and then, as soon as you get to know them, you leave."

It should be pointed out again that each of these young men was achieving real success in his work. There was no question that they liked their work, nor that they were rewarded and satisfied in doing it. These feelings of distress with the temporary quality of their work surfaced while they were successfully and actively involved in their work. They surfaced not because of failure in work but because of stress in relationships, what we have referred to as an intimacy crisis. The issue, and we repeat that it is the common and critical issue for the beginning priest, is the unfamiliarity and discomfort with new kinds of human relationships. The service-oriented nature of their human contacts, the lack of intimacy, and the fact of distance are all unfamiliar and uncomfortable. The task-oriented side of the work does not ordinarily present great problems, but the human side of the work is a major problem.

Associated with and usually following upon the feelings of impermanence are feelings of powerlessness. Feeling helpless and ineffectual, and seeing situations calling for some response but being unable to do anything about them, are different ways of speaking of this powerlessness. Father N spoke of a difficulty he was having with one of his co-workers. He said that there was nothing he could do about it, "I just can't get through to him." Father C expressed a desire to help in establishing a greater sense of community in the rectory and began to feel quite ineffectual when he saw that this was not happening. Father S, feeling equally ineffectual in his work, began to wonder whether his ministry was worth anything.

This experience of powerlessness usually stands in contrast to the anticipation of effectiveness with which the new priest enters his work. Ordinarily he will begin with very high self-expectations in the area of pastoral and personal effectiveness. He has been told that he should be a good counselor, a good confessor, a good teacher, a good preacher, a good liturgist, and a good administrator. He has been given courses to train him in these areas and he expects that he can bring about change and results quickly and effectively. Further, he expects not only that he will be proficient in these areas, but that proficiency will bring a sense of personal reward.

The reality does not fulfill the promise. His ministry does not bring about magical changes in the lives of his people. His work may be quite effective, but it is not effective in the way he had anticipated. His anticipations have an almost magical quality to them. But the results and effectiveness appear to come as the result of thoughtful and hard work, much as they would in a secular area, and have little of the special quality he had anticipated, little of the magical powers he appeared to expect. It appears to be the lack of the anticipated special quality, not the lack of results, that brings about self-doubts which are both common and troubling.

Further, they prove to be self-doubts. Although focused on the work situation, or on the living situation, these self-doubts do not surface because of ineffectiveness but because of a feeling of powerlessness in that situation, which is different. Each of the priests mentioned above, when questioned about his situation, responded that it was not objectively bad. But it was not what he had anticipated and he felt powerless to bring about what he wanted. As a result, his feelings about himself, and especially about himself in relationship to the work, underwent a change. It no longer felt like the supportive and personally rewarding situation he had anticipated. It is as though he were saying. "Since the magic didn't work, maybe the life won't be so happy either."

In short, these considerations of disillusionment, of powerlessness and impermanence point to one central question: What kind of human relationships does a priest have? Implicitly or explicitly, this question is raised by the beginning priest, and is raised in a crisis situation. Our experience teaches that he needs help in understanding what the nature of this crisis is and also in understanding his way of dealing with the crisis. This experience of disillusionment is the critical surfacing of the intimacy crisis in the life of the beginning priest. Left to resolve this by himself, he may reach a destructive resolution, as the numbers of young priests leaving their ministry indicates. But even though his personal strengths and resources may allow him to survive we can anticipate that the very fact of having resolved a relational problem alone will affect his

141

view of the way the relational issues are to be resolved. If, on the other hand, he should be given help in working through this critical issue he will learn that people, working together, can address themselves successfully to relational questions. Should the assistance he receives come from the Church itself, especially from another priest, the possibilities of learning through modeling are considerable. He can learn that a pastor can be of real assistance at a time of personal crisis through the simple method of having experienced crisis himself.

Adjustment from the life of the seminarian to the life of the priest, as we have seen, proves to be very difficult. The difficulty is magnified by the frequently conflicting messages given the priest as he begins his work. These difficulties reach their fullest development in that period of stress which we call the intimacy crisis. The successful resolution to this crisis, which means learning how to establish pastorally effective and personally satisfying relationships, proves to be the major assistance in helping the beginning priest assume a true role of pastoral leadership.